New Urban
Environments

New Urban Environments

British Architecture
and its European Context

Edited by

Peter Murray and MaryAnne Stevens

Prestel

Munich · New York

Published on the occasion of the exhibition
'New Urban Environments: British Architecture
and its European Context'
Park Tower Hall (Shinjuku Park Tower) Shinjuku, Tokyo, and
Hiroshima City Museum of Contemporary Art, 1998, and,
subsequently, at other venues

This exhibition is presented in association with the
Japan UK Festival '98 and has been supported by the
Drue Heinz Trust

Co Curators: Peter Murray and MaryAnne Stevens

Front Cover: Richard Rogers Partnership,
The Millennium Experience, Greenwich
Photography: Hayes Davidson (montage)

Prestel-Verlag
Mandlstrasse 26 · 80802 Munich · Germany
Tel. (+49 89) 38 17 09 0; Fax (+49 89) 38 17 09 35
and 16 West 22nd Street, New York, NY 10010, USA
Tel. (212) 627 8199; Fax (212) 627 9866

Prestel books are available worldwide.
Please contact your nearest bookseller or write to either of
the above addresses for infomation concerning your local
distributor.

Design and layout by WIGEL, Munich
Lithography by ReproLine, Munich
Printed and bound by Passavia Druckerei, Passau
Printed in Germany on acid-free paper

ISBN 3-7913-1937-X

New Urban Environments: British Architecture and its European Context represents the fourth major exhibition created in recent years by the Royal Academy of Arts and devoted to the achievements of contemporary British architects. Presaged by *The New Architecture: Foster, Rogers and Stirling* (1986), *Contemporary British Architecture* (1995–96) and *Living Bridges* (1996), this exhibition specifically explores the achievement of contemporary British architects to create buildings of great aesthetic and functional distinction within established, and frequently comprehensively preserved, urban environments. The issues which the architects have to address, ranging from urban context to ecological responsibility, have informed the design solution to the extent that they have produced buildings and large-scale plans of considerable distinction. Such issues, debates and ultimate solutions would appear to be of increasing relevance worldwide. Mindful of this, the Royal Academy of Arts, as an institution committed to the open debate and careful consideration of such matters, chose to create an exhibition which both presented beautifully resolved architectural solutions and raised issues of public and professional concern.

To achieve such an exhibition has been the result of a close and fruitful collaboration. It has been selected and curated by Peter Murray, Director of Wordsearch Communications, with MaryAnne Stevens, Education Secretary and Chief Curator at the Royal Academy, ably assisted in the preliminary stages by Corinne Wellesley. The exhibition has been organised by Linda Brown and designed by Michael Stiff of Stiff & Trevillion Architects. The mounting of the exhibition in Japan has been masterminded by our associates, Delphi Inc., ably led by its President, Yoshiteru Kaneko. The presentation of the exhibition in Japan has been made possible through the energy and vision of the Organising Committee, expertly chaired by Toshio Yamazaki, to whom we not only owe an enormous debt of gratitude for the time which he has devoted to making this project such a success, but also for his commitment to ensuring the support of so impressive a list of sponsors, both in Tokyo and in Hiroshima. As Chairman of the Japanese Committee of Honour of the Royal Academy of Arts, Toshio Yamazaki has also brought to the project the full support of the members of that committee. Finally, we must underscore the great generosity of All Nippon Airways (ANA), who have provided magnificent support for both personnel working on the exhibition and for the transportation of the exhibition to Japan.

The Royal Academy of Arts conveys its gratitude to all those who have contributed to the successful realization of this project. We are confident that visitors to the exhibition will have the opportunity both to study and enjoy the individual works and consider the broader issues raised within it, concerning the relationship between excellence in contemporary architectural design and the future of our urban environments.

Sir Philip Dowson CBE
President
Royal Academy of Arts, London

A Creative Dialogue:

Contemporary British Architecture and the Urban Environment

Robert Maxwell

This exhibition is not intended to be a mere summary of current British architecture, since not all the protagonists are British. Rather a collection of buildings that corresponds closely to current British attitudes towards architectural design. The dominant quality of these buildings is a sense of empirical reality. British culture has had the bias for centuries, since William of Occam wielded his axe, or at least since Sir Isaac Newton inveighed against the continental taste for making hypotheses. Hypotheses might have intellectual interest, but their fate was to succumb to facts. Newton was supremely oblivious to the fact that his own discoveries were based on intuitions that performed the role of hypotheses in his own thinking. This "preference" for the facts is paralleled by Dr. Johnson's conviction that a bad argument can be demolished by simply referring to the facts; on one occasion in conversation with a critic he asserted, "Sir, I refute you thus", kicking away a stone in his path.

To this cultural prejudice of the British we can add a modern chapter: modern architecture of the twentieth century was not invented in Britain, in spite of the huge contribution made by Charles Rennie Mackintosh, but by European continentals, such as Jacobus J. P. Oud and Le Corbusier. However, functionalism as a creed was exactly to British taste. By appealing to function as a basis for form, one could evade responsibility for the artistic outcome, and claim to be justified by the facts.

Functionalism was adopted wholeheartedly by British architects from the 1950s onwards, and the attitude that it embodies was most succinctly expressed by the British critic Reyner Banham. His programmatic use of the term, maintained through voluminous writings over nearly fifty years, became the basis for contemporary architecture in Britain. His enjoyment of empirical facts, the "nuts and bolts" of construction, led him to promote the Archigram Group, which depicted buildings purely as mechanisms; after the group's participation in Expo '70 in Osaka with the help of Arata Isozaki, this

influence became global, at least among students. Some junior Archigramists moved into the office of Richard Rogers, and contributed to the nuts and bolts of the Centre Pompidou in Paris. In Archigram, a liberating fantasy was an important ingredient, and this may account for the fact that most of their work remained on paper. Yet in some ways the architecture of Richard Rogers can be regarded as buildable Archigram, a performance that certainly embodies a lot of what was originally promised.

In terms declared by Reyner Banham, promise and performance were not synonymous, although of equal importance for good design. A failed performance could be rectified in a subsequent design, while a failed promise was perfidious, and morally reprehensible. In some way, a failed promise suggested a susceptibility towards appearance in place of actuality, or a preference of form over content. An Italian – Lodoli – had made the case at the end of the 18th century for functional performance once and for all. In spite of his admiration for modem Italian design, Banham suspected it of being obsessed with style, a tendency that led inexorably towards the sin of formalism.

True functionalism was premised on rejecting formalism, concentrating on result, and escaping from style altogether. Following Banham's precepts, emphasising what looks good, but only if "it works", British design has retained a strong empiricist base, and as a result the ability to reconcile appearance and actuality may be regarded as a British strength. In the era of the all-powerful image, British architects are known to be mindful of the efficacy of science and technology. Paradoxically, this has resulted in the perception that "high-tech" design is an architectural style.

Other European cultures have produced examples of scientific design, usually developed from structural analysis – as in the case of the Italians Pier Luigi Nervi and Renzo Piano, or the Spaniard Santiago Calatrava.

Pier Luigi Nervi, Palace of Labour, Turin
(Photography: Erno Goldfinger, Architectural Association
Photo Library)

No other European country has wanted to make engineering design a constituent part of ordinary building; neither France, where the polytechnics are an accepted part of the cultural horizon, nor in Germany, where architectural qualification is considered to be a branch of engineering. Compared with these educational traditions, the British tradition is more varied, less dogmatic, and less systematic. One is tempted to conclude that what really motivates the British is the tradition of the gifted amateur, and that the British adoption of technology, not so much as the workings of scientific law but rather as a game plan providing openings to a providential opportunity, has allowed them to become fully enamoured of technology. British architects view technology not as a central institution in encompassing the rule, but from outside, from its margins, as a practical way of avoiding social rules and hence of evading normal outcomes. In this way it becomes a form of play. Through this it may be said that the British have indeed invented the high-tech style.

By the accident of alphabetical order, the material reviewed for this exhibition produced a solid sequence of high-tech designing from Farrrell through Foster and Future Systems, to Grimshaw and after a gap, to Hopkins and finally Rogers. Within this sequence, Terry Farrell is something of an exception: he started out as a partner with Nicholas Grimshaw, but has diverged somewhat by way of an interest in symbolic form and city context. He can, however, summon up the high-tech look whenever he thinks it appropriate. The others all espouse the hands-on approach that asks the question, "how does it work?" before the question, "how does it look?"

That this has become a settled approach in Britain is shown by the emergence of a new generation with similar preferences: Armstrong Architects, David Marks and Julia Barfield, Nick Derbyshire, Stephen Hodder. Lifschutz Davidson, Ian Ritchie and Chris Wilkinson all

Chris Wilkinson, South Quay Bridge
(Photography: Morley von Sternberg)

show proficiency in their use of industrial components, but also a pleasing variety in the personal use they make of similar material. As Charles Jencks has noted, in Britain high-tech architecture may now be seen as the preference of the architectural establishment. It is also a testament to the teaching and influence of Reyner Banham, about whom Colin Rowe, from a dialectically opposite viewpoint has said: "It is Banham's strength to be the possessor of a crucial and simple idea. ... he continues to believe that modern architecture ... can be exactly what it was claimed to be, i.e. an objective approach to building deriving from the unprejudiced scrutiny of the facts". It seems then that Banham has bequeathed this crucial and simple idea to an entire generation, and that it is the conviction of having direct access to "the facts" that empowers British architecture today.

One result of this approach is the tendency to see the individual building as a crafted machine, well detailed and smoothly articulated, but held somewhat in isolation from its immediate environment. Modern architecture grew in the atmosphere of the machine aesthetic, and so tended to produce a succession of well-crafted objects, surrounded by inarticulate space. Historically this approach has been credible in terms of individual buildings, but less successful when we consider the aggregate effect of buildings set within the city. There has been little recognition of the space between buildings, and still less of the metaphysical space that lies between individual building design and the design, or management, of whole sectors of the city.

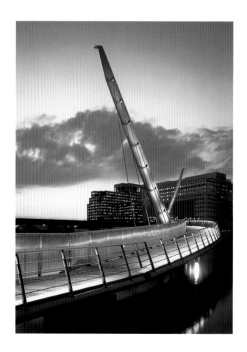

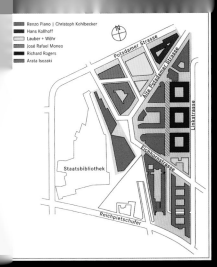

In order to create variety within a prescribed format, the services of an international band of architects has been employed on the Potsdamer Platz masterplan. A desire to mimic the variety of older cities, which have changed in the course of time, is a characteristic of post-modern urban planning.

Daimler-Benz Offices and Housing | Architect **Richard Rogers Partnership** (Photography: Eamonn O'Mahony)

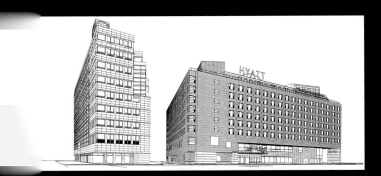

Office Buildings, Potsdamer Platz | Architect **Arata Isozaki & Associates and Steffen Lehmann & Partner** (Photography: Vincent Mosch)

The two buildings arise from a trapezoidal site at the south end of the Daimler-Benz complex. The 7m-high buildings are arranged in a linear row extending in a north-south direction and enclose a public garden, with five bridges connecting the two sides. The aim was to find an appropriate extension for the existing sequence of buildings along the channel as established by Fahrenkamp, Stirling, Mies and Scharoun.

Potsdamer Platz Masterplan | Architect **Renzo Piano**

Hotel and Office Building, Potsdamer Platz | Architect **Rafael Moneo Architects**

Given the prescribed heights and building lines of the Renzo Piano masterplan for Potsdamer Platz, it was difficult to avoid the typological structure of a hotel – a double ring of rooms served by a common corridor. The scheme for the public areas is derived from an analysis of the surrounding urban fabric highlighting the access points. A generous staircase ensures spatial continuity between ground and first floors so that the ballroom is almost an extension of the lobby. The exterior walls are transparent to the point of becoming a 'grid', leaving no doubt as to the building type. The lightness of the office building's volume was conceived as a counterpoint to the solid mass of the hotel.

It is fascinating to see this awareness of complex urban space defined as long ago as 1960 in Banham's essay "Stocktaking", in which he allows that a true scientific history would include everything known, and never discard what was ideologically unpalatable, and in which he acknowledges that, contrary to current perception, the city – the mark of a civilised society – could not be constructed without in some way crossing the boundary between technology and innovation and tradition.

Banham's essays note what he identified as an inherent contradiction in post-war man's expectation of the city: most citizens expect to be able to drive straight down an Autoroute de l'Ouest, straight through an Arc de Triomphe and into a Champs Elysées that still has the urbanity of a sequence from Gigi. They demand suburban expansiveness, and urban compactness, ancient monuments and tomorrow's mechanical aids simultaneously and in the same place. They get neither, because on the one hand there is a tradition which cannot be expanded to deal with new developments without disintegrating, and on the other a disorderly pressure of new developments whose effect – because they are competitive and lack an integrating discipline – is disruptive anyhow.

In the 1970s the conviction of being in possession of all the facts began to waver among European architects, and architects like Aldo Rossi began to call attention to the problems of the city, and to recognise that the scope of total design (in Walter Gropius's terms) did not imply an extension to include design to the entire city. For in Europe, the demands of the city are less easy to deny than in the United States or on the Pacific rim, where empty space cries out to be filled. In Europe it is not so easy to find space to fill. Thus European architects have begun to respond to the problem that Banham was so prescient in recognising nearly forty years ago: combining expansiveness with compactness.

Foremost in this development must be the German experience in Berlin. Following the work of the IBA, which began in the 1970s, there was an attempt to extend Berlin by extending its street pattern. This has resulted in a tight control over new development; in the view of many architects an excessive control that denies individual creativity. One aspect of this dialectic resulted in

plans for the development of Friedrichstrasse as a traditional shopping street, where a building by the radical French Architect Jean Nouvel is reduced to just one small episode on the way; on the other hand, the Potsdamer Platz, laid out according to a structure plan by Renzo Piano, is taking shape as the largest single development in Europe, where the Daimler-Benz buildings by Arata Isozaki are also reduced to being one large episode on the way.

In contrast to the over planning of Berlin, the recent development of Barcelona as the city of the Olympic games produced a remarkable result, not by restructuring the entire city, but by demonstrating that the addition of a large number of new buildings could regenerate the city without disrupting it. So we have reached the era when modern architecture no longer insists on universal utopia, but can demonstrate a capacity to fit into an existing city and transform it from within.

In London, the concept of the insertion of significant modern buildings into an old or urban fabric presents an extreme case history of piecemeal development. The system of awarding resources from the National Lottery for projects deemed important has resulted in a design boom (powered by the prospect of a new millennium) that will transform London in a few years entirely through an accumulation of individual building initiatives. London will remain a highly diverse place; although it did not have the benefit of central planning under the recent Conservative Government, to a degree it has benefited from their laissez-faire policies. When all that has so far been imagined has indeed been constructed, it will be a more efficient, and perhaps a more genial city.

One of the most powerful influences in allowing modern architecture to adapt to its place in the city, rather than expecting the city to make way for total design, has been the work of Norman Foster. If his designs occupy a large place in this exhibition it is because he has been

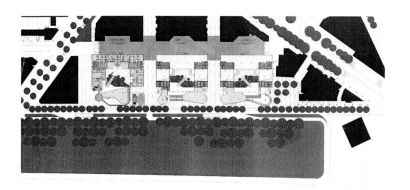

Richard Rogers Partnership, Daimler-Benz Offices and Housing, Potsdamer Platz, Berlin, site plan

For many years Britain suffered from a paucity of new arts-related buildings, but today the funding available from the National Lottery has created a building boom which matches that of the *grands projets* of Paris and the cultural programmes of the traditionally more generous European nations.

Cité de la Musique Est, Paris | Architect **Atelier Christian de Portzamparc**
(Photography: Nicholas Borel)

At the southern entrance to the park of La Villette, the City of Music comprises two complementary yet highly differentiated wings that face each other on either side of the Grande Halle. To the west is the conservatory of music; to the east a complex of public spaces comprising a concert hall, a museum of music, an amphitheatre, rehearsal rooms and administrative offices. The whole forms a series of highly varied projects in a small 'city' formed by distinct volumes set into an overall geometrical form.

The 800-1200-seat concert hall forms the heart of the City's evolving triangular volume – it constitutes the epicentre of a vast spiralling foyer lit by a long glass roof. A covered gallery beneath a long metal girder runs the whole length of the wing defining a labyrinthine promenade.

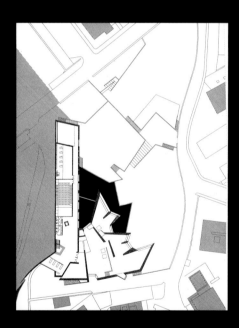

Pilar & Joan Miró Foundation, Palma De Mallorca | Architect **Rafael Moneo**
(Photography: Duccio Malagambs)

It was Joan Miró's express wish to create a study centre for scholars and artists in the city that was his home, as well as a venue for the exhibition and conservation of private collections. The project proposes to establish an uninterrupted dialogue with the pre-existing elements – the studio, the house, topography and, its fundamental piece, the garden. The gallery presents itself as an indefinable and broken space, creating an atmosphere true to the spirit of the paintings. Gaps between the walls are wide or narrow, controlling the amount of direct natural light. Visitors enter at the highest level, from where they descend to three different levels, all related to each other in the definition of the whole.

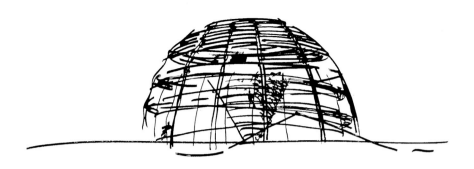

Foster and Partners, New German Parliament, Reichstag, Berlin, roof structure

prominent in leading architecture back to the city from its easier and less demanding placement in what the Americans have romanticised as "Edge City". He has not rejected the opportunity to adapt existing buildings to new conditions (as with the British Museum in London and the Reichstag in Berlin); he has also shown how site limitations can become a source of architectural form. His masterplan for King's Cross is exemplary in this respect – the triangular site becoming the instigation for a wonderful space made up of elegant triangular structures.

If the so-called high-tech is a predominant influence in current British architecture, it is not the only one. Apart from Terry Farrell's highly personal blend of technological and semiological aspects, there are a number of distinguished designers who have demonstrated that starting from site conditions and social considerations does not pre-empt the production of good modern architecture. Daniel Libeskind's Boilerhouse additions for the Victoria and Albert Museum in London are, of course, a *tour de force*. The city will absorb it as successfully as it has his equally uncompromising building for the Jewish Museum in Berlin. Colin St. John Wilson's design for the British Library is informed as much by its place in the city as for its role as a container of books, and the contrast with Perrault's Bibliothèque Nationale could not more clearly express the influence of national culture on modern design.

Finally, in the work of Michael Wilford we see a method, developed over the years of his collaboration with James Stirling, of balancing the demands of function and city form with superlative judgement. Equally impressive here are the designs for the British Embassy in Berlin and the Abando Interchange in Bilbao. In bringing Stirling's last design to completion – the city building at No. 1 Poultry in London – Wilford has demonstrated that building in the city can go beyond current ideologies and stylistic fashions. This building is remarkable in claiming to be at once contemporary and a match for the most distinguished traditional buildings that surround it on all sides. It proclaims the continuation of a tradition of architecture. Given that Stirling claimed to be a functionalist throughout his career, we may take this instance to mark the point where functionalism has come of age.

The current practice of European Architects within the urban setting has contributed to the debate concerning the necessary cohabitation of the traditional with the new; within the city, an issue of increasingly critical significance to the wholesale redevelopment and explosive growth of so many Asian cities. While accepting the tight constraints of the traditional European city, European architects have proposed, with noted success, that modern architecture is no longer restricted by urban planning dogma, but rather can become a vehicle of aesthetic expression and for urban regeneration, and a means to achieve a redefinition of an acceptable multi-layered, historically multi-faceted built environment.

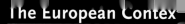

Library at the Universidad Nacional de Educación a Distancia, Madrid
Architect **José Ignacio Linazasoro**
(Photography: Javier Azurmendi)

The library acts as a kind of watch-tower, a gate into the University campus. The fact that it is on a busy traffic route led to the decision to enclose the building. The entrance passageway is at the end of a grand hall with large columns, located on the ground floor and separated from the interior by a glass enclosure. On the ground floor is the card catalogue area, a space for consulting current journals and a computer room, and the second floor is a large open hall serving as a prelude to the next five floors, each specialised according to subject. A cone-shaped atrium slices through the four upper floors, producing a central light-filled space.

The new British Library was completed in 1997 after a gestation period of nearly thirty years. The Bibliothèque Nationale de France was conceived and built in four. Despite their similar completion dates, the two buildings reflect the disparity in their dates of conception. Linzasoros Madrid Library, by comparison, has a timeless quality that characterises this particular trait of European rational design.

Bibliothèque Nationale de France, Paris | Architect and engineer **Perrault Associés SA**
(Photography: George Fessy)

The Bibliothèque Nationale de France is built on a stretch of industrial waste land on the banks of the Seine in the East End of Paris and represents the starting-point for a complete restructuring of this sector of the 13th arrondissement. In an operation designed to redeem this part of the city, the Bibliothèque Nationale de France will exert a new aesthetic and regenerative influence on an area blighted by the Porte de Choisy and Porte d'Ivry high-rise tower-blocks. With its four corner towers resembling four open books facing one another, the Bibliothèque Nationale de France imposes its presence and identity on the scale of the city by the immense size of these corners. The library is organised around a public square, planted with pine trees, which sits behind and below a wood-decked, acropolis-like plinth from which the four towers rise. The top square is similar in size to the Place de la Concorde while the sunken "forest" courtyard at the scheme's heart is of the same dimensions as that

Royal Crescent, Bath – a prime example of a humanist urban approach (Photography: Peter Jeffree, Architectural Association Photo Library)

Richard Burdett

Architecture, like other art forms in Britain, is experiencing an unprecedented period of vibrancy and international recognition. This exhibition is the first of its kind to celebrate the work of a new generation of British architects which is setting new standards in environmental and urban design in Europe today. The aim of the exhibition is to stimulate thought and discussion on the future of the city as it faces a period of intense challenge and epochal change.

The 90 projects included in the show reveal a depth and breadth of architectural creativity that defies categorisation into fashionable styles. There are high-tech office towers, neo- and late-modernist public buildings, deconstructivist arts and performance spaces, and expressionist leisure and sports palaces. There is a fascination with building technology and a passion for innovation. Yet, these diverse strategies are unified by an interest in two fundamental issues: the city and the environment.

The quality of the urban environment is a major concern of the late 20th century. In part it is a question of quantity. Over half the world's population lives in cities (a century ago it was 10%). At a global level, urban growth is increasing at a rate of a quarter of a million people per day – roughly equivalent to a new Tokyo every two months.

However it is also a question of quality. Cities are the setting for increased social inequality and poverty and they are the driving force of the global environmental crisis. Cities are the major destroyers of the eco-system and the greatest threat to our survival on the planet. They consume over 75% of the world's energy and are responsible for a vast proportion of global pollution. Many of the projects in this exhibition recognise the significance of these urban and environmental issues. Behind the different forms of architectural expression is a growing recognition that architecture is a social art, and that architects have a clear social and environmental

responsibility to address the pressing needs of contemporary society: health, well-being, social inequality, financial stability, energy, transport and the environment. In short, they have to address the key issues affecting the quality of life of individual citizens in the urban environment.

This humanist approach is rooted in the town planning tradition of 18th-century England, which the architectural historian Sir John Summerson defined as quintessentially "empirical, ... a happy collision of intent and circumstance". The elegant urban terraces, streets and crescents of Georgian London, the landscaped parks and squares of Edinburgh and Bath are prime examples of a humanist urban approach grounded in economic and social reality.

John Nash and his contemporaries were both imaginative and practical. They created new parts of cities – real estate developed with private money – that responded to the needs of the 'market' with solutions of the highest design content and a strong commitment to the public realm. Regency London and Georgian Bath are beautiful and functional set-pieces of urban theatre which achieve a balance between public and private needs. Buildings are not conceived as objects in isolation but as an integral element of a sequence of well-defined open spaces that establish the public realm of the city.

The public domain, the space between buildings, is the priority that provides continuity in the European urban tradition. Baron Hausmann's 19th-century comprehensive plan for Paris – with its tree-lined boulevards, formal parks and gardens, unified building heights and continuous roof lines – is one version of this urban model. In Berlin, the standardised urban block (200 metres by 80 metres) provides a variation on the theme that defines the streets and public squares. These are cities with a clear geometric logic that has withstood the ravages of war and political division.

It is significant that many of the current projects return to the urban themes of the past albeit with a modern aesthetic. The by-product of social and environmental consciousness has been a rediscovery of 18th- and 19th-century planning models, modernised and upgraded to respond to the needs of the car, public transport and changing lifestyles. The Germans have returned to the 'urban block' as the backbone of the urban reconstruction initiated under the IBA projects of the 1980s – a debate epitomised by the history of the Potsdamer Platz featured in the exhibition. The French have intervened in the traditional city with a series of architectural statements or *grands projets* – the Grande Arche at La Défense, the Très Grande Bibliothèque and the new towns at Marne-la-Vallée or Bercy – that are attempts to extend 19th-century Paris into the 21st century.

It is no coincidence that these cities have been able to adapt to momentous change and development without losing their intrinsic urban qualities. London, Paris and Berlin have remained centres of civic decency throughout the last two hundred years – from the early days of the Industrial Revolution to the Post-Industrial Age. While each nation has created variations on the theme of urban space, it is the equilibrium between public and private that has contributed to their lasting success as models of urban living. The typically British Georgian street and Georgian house, for example, are symbols of continuity and change, adapting easily from the lifestyle of an 18th-century gentleman and his family to the very

modern needs of a computerised office environment. Central to this flexibility is the ability to respond to constraints – a very British characteristic that sets this urban tradition apart from the grand gestures of French and German town planning.

It could be argued that this pragmatic town planning approach was a precursor of the 'long-life-loose-fit-low-cost' school that has so strongly influenced British design since the 1960s. This slogan, originally adopted as a battle cry by the proto 'high-tech' architects of the 1960s, called for a more flexible approach to design that liberated architecture from the formalist shackles of pure modernism.

The current generation of architects featured in the exhibition have enriched this tradition with an environmental and urban agenda that accounts for its new-found vibrancy. Curved roof profiles, thinner and leaner building forms, articulated plans that respond to orientation and solar exposure, vertical features that act as thermal chimneys and tall atrium spaces that function as air plenums are the recognisable features of a new architectural language. A language that cuts across conventional stylistic categories.

At the urban level there are similar consistencies. Buildings are designed to face the street, provide continuity and access to the public realm. There is a move away from the object building, surrounded by empty space.

Inken & Hinrich Baller, IBA Housing, Berlin (Photography: Hazel Cook, Architectural Association Photo Library)

Johan O. von Spreckelson, La Grande Arche, Paris (Photography: Pat Charlesworth, Architectural Association Photo Library)

Lifschutz Davidson, Oxo Tower, London (Photography: Timothy Soar)

Transparency and permeability establish a direct relationship between buildings and their urban surroundings, creating safer and more humane urban environments.

However, the path taken by recent large schemes that have incorporated these ideas has not always been smooth. Paternoster Square, for instance, next to St Paul's Cathedral, has been awaiting redevelopment since the early 1980s. A competition among a group of international architects inlcuding Arata Isozaki, Richard Rogers, Norman Foster and Arup Associates was held in 1987. Arup's won, but their scheme was heavily criticised by HRH The Prince of Wales and a neoclassical design, masterplanned by Terry Farrell, was proposed instead. This also failed because of a slump in the property market. As the market recovered it became clear that neoclassical buildings were unlettable to the international banks and lawyers who would occupy office space on this site, and a new plan designed by William Whitfield with buildings by Richard MacCormac, Michael Hopkins and Allies and Morrison is now under consideration.

Another major London development that has spent more than a decade on the drawing boards is King's Cross. Part of the site is occupied by King's Cross and St Pancras railway stations, destined to become the terminus for trains using the Channel Tunnel. The area behind the stations, a vaste hinterland of rail tracks, wasteland and historic industrial buildings, was also the subject of a competition. A number of architects including Terry Farrell and Skidmore Owings & Merrill took part with the result that Norman Foster designed a masterplan which included the provision of a large park in the centre of the space, new office buildings straddling the railway lines and a dramatic triangular new terminal next to the existing stations. However, the local authority failed to give the project planning permission; this, combined with the effects of a slump in the office market, meant that the developers threw in the towel.

On a smaller scale, attitudes to urbanism are changing. In recent years London has witnessed a dramatic increase in living accommodation in the centre of the city. As a result of the same recession that crippled the large scale developments, owners of older commercial properties realised that it was more profitable to turn them into lofts and apartments than to let them as

offices or workshops. The planning authorities allowed the use of these buildings to change at the same time as demand for mid-urban residential accommodation grew. This growth has coincided with a general enthusiasm for the metropolis, for pavement cafés, late night shopping, grand scale, high-quality restaurants and a desire to ameliorate the urban environment which is typified by the small scale, but highly influential project by CZWG for a public lavatory-cum-florist in Notting Hill Gate.

Two hundred years on, John Summerson's 'collision of intent and circumstance' can be seen to be alive today, underpinning the work of a wide range of emerging and established designers. The exhibition offers a unique view – a genuine cross-section – of British design at the end of the 20th century against the backdrop of contemporary European practice.

Terry Farrell and Partners
King's Cross Masterplan, London

Foster and Partners
King's Cross Masterplan, London

Arup Associates
Paternoster Square, London

Foster and Partners
Paternoster Square, London

CZWG Architects
Bankside Lofts, London

CZWG Architects
Brindleyplace Café, Birmingham

CZWG Architects
Westbourne Grove Public Lavatory and
Island Landscaping, London

Lifschutz Davidson
South Bank Riverside Walkway, London

The Post-Modern City

Two major, large-scale planning exercises of the past ten
years, the masterplans for King's Cross and Paternoster
Square, illustrate attempt by architects and planners to
develop a new urban vocabulary. While maintaining
some of the existing historical structure of their
surroundings, respecting the street and public space,
these projects have had to deal with the large-scale
requirements of modern business.

A solution for the Paternoster Square scheme, for which
a series of designs has been proposed since 1987, is at
last in sight. A masterplan by Sir William Whitfield
incorporates designs by a number of different architects
– a similar strategy to that employed at Potsdamer Platz.
The desire to create variety is satisfied by the use of
different styles.

At the other end of the scale, a celebration of urbanism
can be seen in the work of CZWG where small-scale
insertions – cafés, florists, lavatories – enhance existing
environments. The growth of loft-living during recent
years in Britain represents a new interest in metropolitan
lifestyle.

The work of Lifschutz Davidson, supported by a strong
local community, has made a significant improvement
to a very ragged area of London. This ability to respect
the existing character of an area, yet insert buildings that
are unashamedly modern, is the essence of the Post-
Modern City.

Terry Farrell and Partners

King's Cross Masterplan, London

The masterplan accommodates office, leisure, residential, retail, transport and community uses on 125 acres of largely derelict British Rail land between King's Cross and St Pancras Stations.

The plan focuses upon the canal as the heart of the scheme and the heritage of the area is reinforced by the retention and re-use of listed buildings, approached from the main road by a new boulevard. Pedestrian, cycle and vehicular circulation is accommodated mainly at ground level, while interchanges for the Channel Tunnel Terminal are provided both here and at lower levels. The existing rail and Underground complexes are improved and better integrated with other uses.

The New King's Cross makes a major addition to London's cityscape, tying in with the surrounding area in a neighbourly, sensitive and appropriate manner. It also provides for a positive, lively, human scale environment in which a variety of architectural forms can be incrementally accommodated, replicating traditional and successful urban change.

This proposal was an entry to the limited competition for the site, won by Foster and Partners.

Client **London Regeneration Consortium**
Architect **Terry Farrell and Partners**
Structural Engineer **Ove Arup & Partners**
M&E Services Engineer **Ove Arup & Partners**
Quantity Surveyor **Gardiner & Theobald**
Programme **1987 (design)**

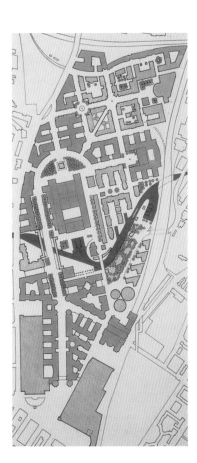

As masterplanners for this vast area, the Foster office created a framework within which more detailed design work could take place. Central to the philosophy has been the need to establish a balanced community. In particular, five considerations gave rise to the organisation of the 52-hectare site: a series of heritage buildings grouped around the historic railway sheds to the south and the canal/road interchange in the centre; the canal itself; the infrastructure of road and rail; the need to break down physical barriers around the site and form intelligible new routes; and the heart of the development, a new open space in the tradition of London's parks and squares.

The new International Terminal, placed between King's Cross and St Pancras Stations, forms a vast triangular structure, with glass and steel roof shells allowing the influx of natural light. The terminal's features include unimpeded lines of sight, clear signing, reduced walking distances and smooth changes in level. The building was designed to give a feeling of space, light and airiness, while housing all the ticketing and retail facilities expected by passengers of the twenty-first century.

This scheme failed to obtain planning permission and was abandoned. The site remains derelict awaiting a revised scheme.

Client **London Regeneration Consortium**
Architect **Foster and Partners**
Structural Engineer **Ove Arup & Partners**
Quantity Surveyor **Davis Langdon & Everest**
Market Research **Baker Harris Saunders**
Traffic Consultants **Halcrow Fox & Associates**
Landscaping **Hanna Olins**
Heritage Issues **Julian Harrap Architects**
Service Engineers **JBB**
Photography **Richard Davies**
Programme **1987 (design)**

Arup Associates

Paternoster Square, London

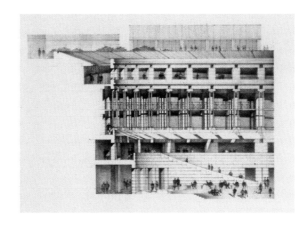

The site, known as Paternoster because of its historical links with and proximity to St Paul's Cathedral, had been redeveloped after the damage of World War II. However, the office blocks which had been built over elevated pedestrian decks were considered inadequate for the current requirements of office users and felt to be inappropriate. Not only were the blocks unrelated to the Cathedral, but the shops were of a poor quality and the public spaces were bleak and uninviting.

In their competition submission, Arup Associates presented a proposal for the whole of the masterplan site which incorporated both office and retail accommodation in a development which could be completed in phases over a period. In addition it made provision for improved facilities for the Cathedral with shops and amenities for visitors as well as a new exit from the Crypt. The plan for Paternoster envisaged approximately 1,250,000 sq. ft of newly built space at ground-floor level and above on the masterplan site. This space would be used for offices and retail purposes and will be planned within a series of new buildings of between four and eight storeys in height. The development consists of about 1,050,000 sq. ft of offices above ground together with 300,000 sq. ft for public uses including restaurants, cafés, pubs and shops. Other uses such as a hotel and a museum could be included within the scheme. In addition, some 225,000 sq. ft of space is occupied by public spaces, the arcade and square, with a further 17,000 sq. ft provided for use by the Cathedral.

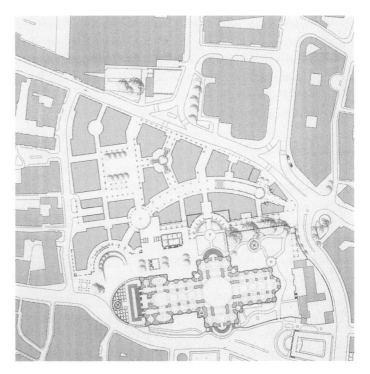

Client **Paternoster Properties NV**

Architect **Arup Associates**

Structural Engineer **Arup Associates**

Quantity Surveyor **Arup Associates**

Project Co-ordinators **The Mountleigh Group**

Project Management **Stanhope Properties plc**

Photography **Peter Mackniven**

Programme **1987 (design)**

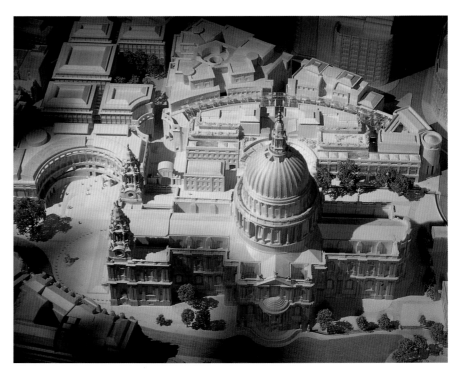

The proposals for the Paternoster precinct were based on an alternating grid of public routes and private courtyards following an earlier project modelled on the casbah, a hierarchical city within a city. The public and private spaces run north-south, at an angle to the main axes of St Paul's Cathedral. Between each route and courtyard are a series of 18m-wide building units with retail space at ground level and offices above. Each unit may be let separately with its own entrance from a private courtyard or may form part of a larger grouping which might even encompass the entire masterplan site.

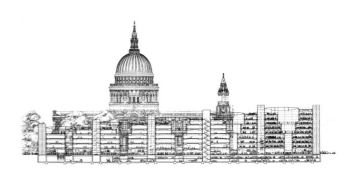

The scheme provides a system which could respond flexibly to commercial and environmental pressures. The buildings terrace downwards from the west to the east in response to the height regulations of the Cathedral. This allows access to generous roof-top courts and gardens. At the southern edge, the development terminates in a colonnade forming a tightly enclosed piazza, in keeping with Wren's original masterplan for the Cathedral precinct.

Client **Paternoster Properties NV**
Architect **Foster Associates**
Civil, Structural & Traffic Engineer **Ove Arup & Partners**
M&E Services Engineer **J. Roger Preston & Partners**
Acoustical Engineer **Tim Smith Acoustics**
Construction Cost **Davis Langdon & Everest**
Photography **Richard Davies**
Programme **1987 (design)**

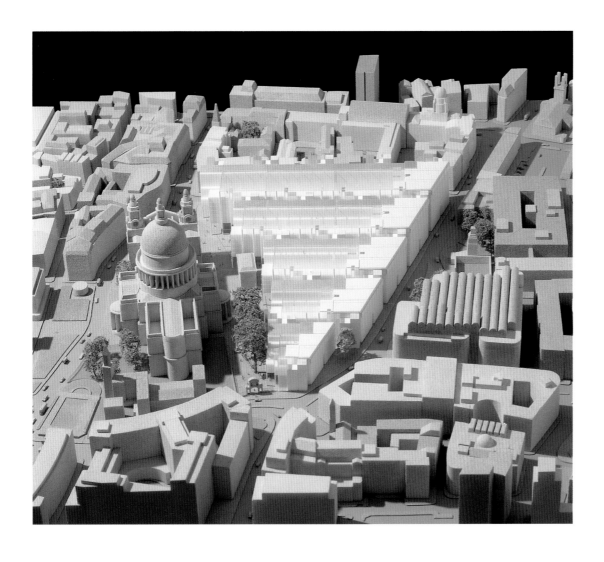

CZWG Architects

Bankside Lofts, London

The popularity of lofts for residential accommodation is a reflection of a new enthusiasm for urban living.

This group of idiosyncratic buildings, the oldest of which is an Italianate red-brick mill, with deep floor-to-ceiling heights, heavy structural beams and columns and differing windows on every floor, makes for perfect loft accommodation. The stepped overall form allows for well-orientated roof terraces. Under the central half-acre garden is a secure underground car park with direct lift access. The building will offer mixed use accommodation, shops and commercial premises on ground and basement levels, including an art gallery. These lofts have a spectacular view of the Tate Gallery, Bankside.

Client **Manhattan Lofts**

Architect **CZWG Architects**

Structural Engineer **Vincent Grant & Partners**

M&E Services Engineer **Envirotemp**

Quantity Surveyor **Leslie Clark & Partners**

Contractor **John Sisk & Son Ltd.**

Perspective Drawing **Andrew Williamson**

Models **3DD**

Photography **Courtesy of Manhattan Lofts**

Programme **Phases 1, 2, & 3 contain 99 flats.**

Phase 4 still under construction and Phase 5 to come.

The Bar Rouge Café, the centrepiece of the new Central Square at Brindleyplace, is an example of the sort of small-scale intervention that enlivens the post-modern city. The eye-shaped building sits over the centre of a radial pattern of York stone which visually links the interior and exterior through the generous glazed doors. It is surrounded by extensive landscaping of semi-mature trees, sculpture, a large water feature and 'sculpted' grassed areas.

Its own structure is sculptural, consisting of a tubular steel frame that is completely glazed. The line of the vertical structural columns is continued to the roof members and cross-over at the ridge to form canopies that mirror the footprint of the building. In response to the vertical scale of the square, the building projects vertically by means of 'butterfly' extensions to the roof glazing. Secure storage and pumping space is provided at basement level hidden from view to maintain the integrity of the transparency of the café.

Client **Argent Group plc**
Architect **CZWG Architects**
Structural Engineer **Kara Taylor**
M&E Services Engineer **Kyle Stewart**
Quantity Surveyor **Silk & Frazier**
Contractor **Kyle Stewart**
Environmental Consultant **Townsend Landscape Architects**
Photography **Chris Gascoigne**
Programme **1996–97**

CZWG Architects

Westbourne Grove Public Lavatory and Island Landscaping, London

The lavatory building, its walls clad in turquoise glazed brick, stands on a new triangular island. Continuous horizontal louvres line the top of the walls to ventilate the internal spaces. The projecting canopy roof is rectangular with a fan-shaped end, and the internal spaces are lit naturally through the translucent covering. The sharp end of the triangle is formed by a glazed brick plinth which is partially enclosed with plate glass to create a flower kiosk – an idea added to the original brief.

The wider end of the building houses the public lavatories which can be entered from either side into an open lobby. This leads to the lavatory for disabled persons and the cleaners' room to one side, with the remainder split into the men's and women's lavatories by a service corridor under the central gutter. This duct is front-ended by the central attendant's kiosk from which the doors to the lavatories and entrances can be seen, as well as having views to the outside. Dancing silhouettes on the steel entrance doors advertise the building's use when the doors are open.

Client **The Royal Borough of Kensington & Chelsea in conjunction with The Pembridge Association**
Architect **CZWG Architects**
Structural Engineer **Dewhurst Macfarlane & Partners**
Quantity Surveyor **Orbell Associates**
Main Contractor **R Mansell Ltd**
Photography **Chris Gascoigne**
Programme **1993**

The international and domestic termini at Waterloo Station make the South Bank a major gateway to London. New connections to the riverside walkway will provide the key link to many of central London's attractions via a traffic-free promenade with outstanding views. Substantial parts of the existing riverside walkway will be demolished and rebuilt in the near future, so it is imperative that a co-ordinated design strategy is agreed upon which can be implemented in phases alongside the programmes of the individual projects.

The South Bank riverside walkway and landscape strategy is not a cosmetic exercise. It will provide a long-term solution to the existing problems of the walkway, will enhance the environment for year-round activity, and will accommodate the large increase in visitor numbers expected. Without a proper strategy the riverside walkway will never achieve the quality and integration that it deserves as one of London's most popular promenades. The strategy proposed envisages the upgrading of the riverside walkway and adjacent areas to create a magnificent public pleasure garden linking both existing and new riverside attractions.

Joint Client **South Bank Employers' Group; London Borough of Lambeth; London Borough of Southwark**
Architect **Lifschutz Davidson Ltd.**
Consulting Engineer **Waterman Environmental**
Cost Consultant **Davis Langdon & Everest**
Construction and Programme Advice **Schal International Management Ltd.**
Landscape Consultant **Charles Funke Associates**
Traffic Consultant **The Denis Wilson Partnership**
Acoustic and Theatre **Bickerdike Allen Partners**
Consultants **Carr and Angier**
Photography **Andrew Putler**
Programme **1997–2000**

Ahrends Burton and Koralek Architects
British Embassy, Moscow

Allies and Morrison Architects
British Embassy, Dublin

Alsop & Störmer
Regional Government Headquarters, Marseille

Terry Farrell and Partners
British Consulate-General and British Council, Hong Kong

Terry Farrell and Partners
International Conference Centre, Edinburgh

Foster and Partners
New German Parliament, Reichstag, Berlin

Future Systems
Hallfield School, London

Hodder Associates
Centenary Building, University of Salford

Michael Hopkins and Partners
The New Parliamentary Building, London

Michael Hopkins and Partners
University of Nottingham Campus Masterplan,
Nottingham

Ian Ritchie Architects
Glass Reception Hall, International Exhibition
Centre, Leipzig

Michael Wilford and Partners
British Embassy, Berlin

Public Buildings

Public buildings – representative of local or central government and its institutions – are highly charged with symbolic content. They are designed to reflect the image of the state, to communicate varying degrees of authority and gravitas, democracy and openness, confidence and stability.

Over the past few years the British government has commissioned a number of new buildings to represent its interests in Russia, Ireland, Germany and Hong Kong. These designs confirm the flexibility of the 'embassy' building type. As designs, they succeed in performing a double – often conflicting – role. Their solidity and gravitas communicate a common message of 'Britishness', yet their varied architectural language responds creatively to different urban and national contexts. These are truly post-modern buildings that respond to post-modern urban conditions. Unlike the neoclassical structures of the colonial period or the white monuments of early 20th-century modernism, this new generation of public building is more subtle and flexible, reflecting a greater concern for content and context that transcends architectural fashion or style.

ABK's 'palazzo on the river' contributes to the Moscow skyline with a very British sense of craft and articulation. Allies & Morrison's crisp masonry building fits neatly into the domestic urban landscape of Dublin, integrating the English concern for nature – the garden – with its building interior. Michael Wilford's competition-winning design for the British Embassy in Berlin respects the external rigour of the city's Baroque urban block, yet creates an internal world of surprise that extends the 18th-century English architectural preoccupation with form and space. Terry Farrell's British Council and Trade Commission in Hong Kong is perhaps the last vestige of a truly European urban tradition, with a building that hugs the street, defining the public space in a clear and unambiguous way.

Even Norman Foster, a master of innovation, bows to the strong historic content of the Reichstag building, the new seat of unified Germany's parliament. A glazed structure, delicately balanced above the old masonry building, communicates a subtle but clear message about tradition, continuity and change. The new grows out of the old. Like other European public buildings, the Reichstag is a metaphor for a new sense of openness and civic participation. These messages can be seen to extend to the new generation of educational buildings in Britain – from primary schools to universities – that reflects a genuine concern for the user whilst responding to the exigencies of context and urban form.

Ahrends Burton and Koralek

British Embassy, Moscow

The site for the new British Embassy is on the Smolenskaya Embankment near the government's White House on the Moscow River. At this point the river has a generous curve, giving the site wide views to the west.

The project comprises the Embassy offices, conference and exhibition areas, staff flats and amenities for the occupants. The major public face of the project to the river is determined by four linked buildings. These vary in height: the office building is the highest and centrally placed in the composition between the existing 1950s blocks of apartments, with the new flats either side. The office building projects eastwards, bisecting the site, and creating a forecourt entrance from Protchny Street on one side and a private garden on the other.

The base of the buildings ties the project into the existing context by the use of a massive, curved, yellow stone wall surmounted by a columned screen. And with a small park with trees between it and the road serves as a continuation of the existing tree line.

The tops of the buildings are strongly linked together by means of a series of timber-screened terraces and copper-covered roofs leading to the crowning curved roof over the offices. Materials and colours have been chosen for their reference to Moscow traditions.

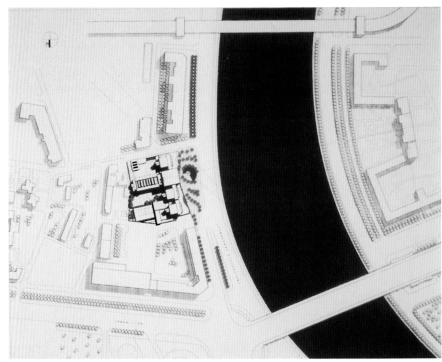

Client **Foreign & Commonwealth Office**
Architect **Ahrends Burton & Koralek**
Structural Engineer **Ove Arup & Partners**
Services Engineer **YME Engineers**
Landscape Consultant **Landesign**
Quantity Surveyor **Hanscomb**
Project Manager **London Group**
Contractor **Taylor Woodrow/Skanska**
Photography **Chris Edgecombe (model)**
Hayes Davidson (montage)
Programme **Completion 1999**

Allies and Morrison Architects

British Embassy, Dublin

The Embassy is designed as a series of interconnecting buildings grouped around an inner courtyard. This cloister-like space provides a central focus for all the activities of the Embassy and recalls the form of many of Dublin's major public buildings. The double-height inner hall overlooking the central courtyard creates a focus for the life of the Embassy.

The individual buildings that together form the courtyard vary in height from one to three storeys, with the highest block accommodating all the main elements of the Embassy, establishing the main public facade onto the street. Like the elevations to the courtyard, this facade is faced in Wicklow granite and further articulated by a trabeated metal grid which, as well as defining the positions of piers and floors, gives support to the roof. The roof itself is decked in natural slate, composed as individual panels set within metal surrounds. The internal organisation of the Embassy is divided into base, *piano nobile* and attic storey. Extensive landscaping has been proposed to establish both an appropriate public forecourt to the Embassy and a relaxed series of garden spaces towards the rear of the site, retaining existing trees wherever possible.

Client **Foreign and Commonwealth Office, Overseas Estates Department**
Architects **Allies and Morrison**
Structural Engineer **Whitby & Bird**
Consulting Structural Engineer **KML Consulting Engineers**
Services Engineer **Max Fordham & Partners**
Consulting Services Engineer **VNRA Consulting Engineers**
Quantity Surveyor **George Corderoy & Co**
Consulting Surveyor **Desmond MacGreevy & Partners**
Landscape Architect **Livingston Eyre Associates**
Consulting Landscape Architect **Mitchell & Associates**
Contractor **Pierce Contracting Ltd**
Photography **Peter Cook, Paul Raftery**
Cost **£6.8m**
Programme **Completion: June 1995**

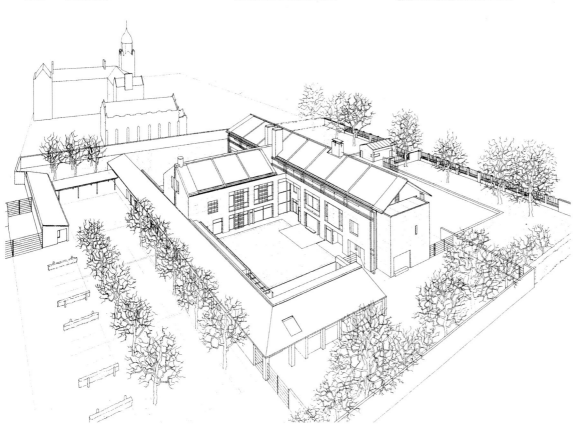

Alsop & Störmer

Regional Government Headquarters, Marseille

For Alsop & Störmer, the commission for the head-quarters of the Département de Bouches-du-Rhône meant an opportunity to put into effect an architectural approach that had been gestating for more than fifteen years, developing themes such as simple linear forms, the invention of radical engineering solutions, and the development of energy efficient prototypes.

The building provides 100,000 sq.m of offices for 1,700 civil servants. The continuity of the state is expressed in the solidity of the two blocks of office space, but is combined with an element of transparency alien to traditional state buildings. The central atrium is a public square that contains several functions; the free-standing elliptical tube in the heart of the building serves as a public exhibition space while the lower floors of the blocks house a library, 'mediathèque' and restaurant. The two elliptical structures visible from outside the building express the democratic functions – the chambers and the councillors' offices.

Client **Conseil Général de Bouches-du-Rhône**
Architect **Alsop & Störmer**
Structural Engineer and Environmental Engineer
Ove Arup & Partners
Project Artists **Bruce McClean, Daniel Buran, Brian Clarke**
Quantity Surveyor **Hascombe**
Technical Consultants **OTH (France)**
Photographer **Paul Raftery**
Cost **£115m**
Programme **1990–96**

Terry Farrell and Partners

British Consulate-General and British Council, Hong Kong

The design concept, resulting in two separate perimeter buildings linked by a common entrance pavilion, was influenced as strongly by urban design as it was by architecture. The two major buildings – the Consulate-General and the British Council – have their own position and identity, providing a long public frontage to Hong Kong and quiet contemplative views to the private, secluded gardens, carefully designed to retain many of the existing trees.

The architectural language establishes a modern, well-tailored, identifiably British scheme which unifies both buildings, and the consistent 10-storey height and roof line echoes the Hong Kong public buildings of the past.

The buildings are constructed of reinforced concrete frames. The main elevations incorporate long, hole-in-wall windows in a masonry-clad wall of white granite. Spandrels to the windows and panelled areas around the entrances are in Kirkstone slate. The elevations to major rooms and principal circulation areas on the street frontages have full-height glazing in clear, anodized aluminium frames.

Client **HM Government, Overseas Estate Department,**
Foreign & Commonwealth Office
Architect **Terry Farrell and Partners**
Structural, M&E and Geotechnical Engineer
Ove Arup & Partners
Quantity Surveyor **Widnell, Hong Kong**
Project Manager **Swire Properties Projects**
Main Contractor **Laing-Hip Hing Joint Venture**
Landscape Architect **Denton Corker Marshall, Hong Kong**
Photography **Peter Cook**
Cost **£60m**
Programme **1992–96**

Terry Farrell and Partners

International Conference Centre, Edinburgh

The design was influenced by the shape of the site, change of levels and the need for a compact design to meet budget restrictions. Also, it forms an important element in Farrell's masterplan, and establishes the set-back and curve on the street frontage to provide for pedestrian access to the newly proposed Conference Square.

A number of massing studies and the outline of the site influenced the shaping of the four lower corner pavilions leading to an overall building design with a simple, strong architecture appropriate both to Scotland and to the international prestige of the Conference Centre. Combined with the prominent roof edge feature, this produces a building with both civic presence and the required image.

In keeping with the masterplan principles, the elevations are of a light buff/grey sandstone colour, traditional to Edinburgh, with a greater solid than void proportion. The four facades each have their own character and detail within an overall architectural concept. Small areas of contrasting stone and strong colour are used for maximum impact which will be enhanced by night-time lighting.

Client **Edinburgh International Conference Centre**
Architect **Terry Farrell and Partners**
Structural and Services Engineer **Ove Arup & Partners, West Lothian**
Quantity Surveyor **Gleeds, Edinburgh**
Main Contractor **GA Management, Edinburgh**
Acoustic and Theatre Design Consultant **Sandy Brown Associates**
Photography **Keith Hunter, Nigel Young**
Cost **£33m**
Programme **1990, 1993–95**

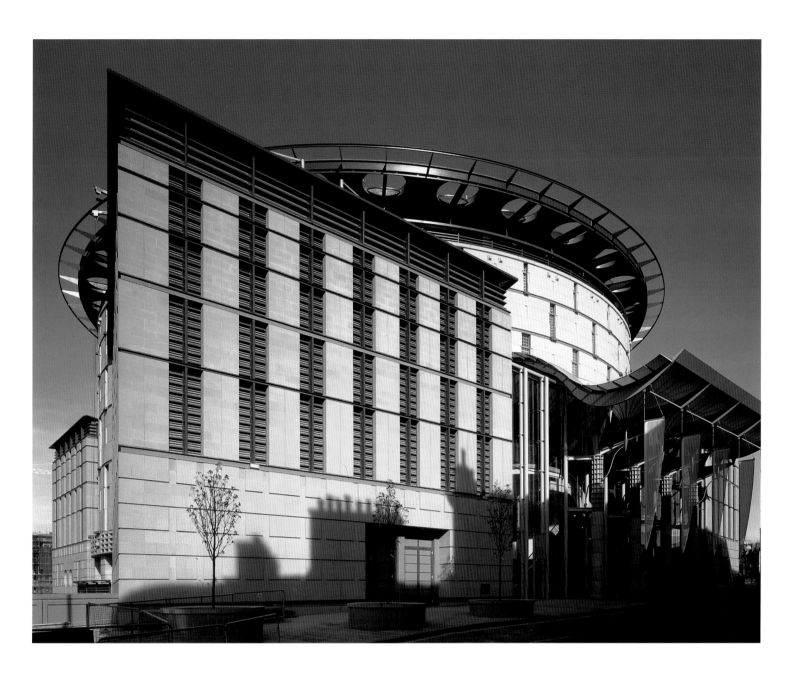

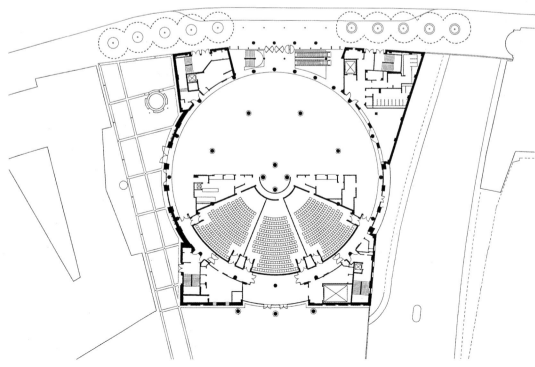

Foster and Partners

New German Parliament, Reichstag, Berlin

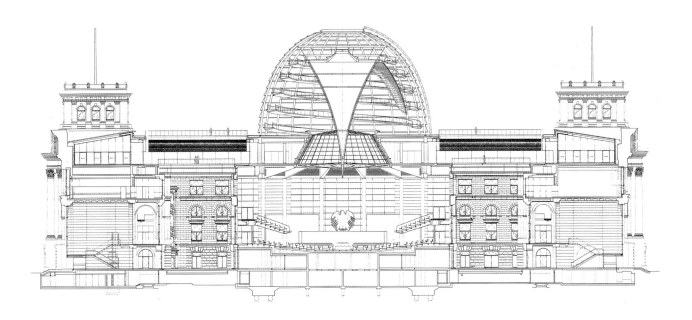

The original design brief was to accommodate the German Parliament in the historic Reichstag building in Berlin. This specified an area of 34,000 sq.m. However, the second competition stage asked for significantly less space. The revised needs were so different it was necessary to draft a new design. The updated proposals are rooted in four major issues – the workings of Parliament, the history of the Reichstag, ecology/energy, and the economics of realising the project.

For the processes of democracy to be revealed, the public areas would have to become a vital part of the revised brief. In this new approach the roof is considered a major public space, and the principal raised entrance level is to be recreated. This allows the grand ceremonial entrance, now blocked up, to be re-opened as a democratic main entrance for everyone. It was decided to make the Reichstag a living museum of German history by peeling away the fabric to reveal traces of the past, such as shell marks, charred timber and graffiti from the period of the Russian occupation.

The final design incorporates a roof structure or cupola, which will deflect controlled daylight into the Plenary Chamber below and also scoop out air as part of the natural ventilation system. The structure will also contain an array of photovoltaic cells as a part of the energy system and provide support for an elevated viewing deck accessed by helical ramps.

Client **Federal Republic of Germany, represented by**
Bundesbaugesellschaft Berlin mbH
Architect **Foster and Partners**
Structural Engineer **Ove Arup & Partners;**
Schlaich Bergermann & Partner
Acoustics **Müller BBM GmbH; Prof. George Plenge**
M&E Services Engineer **Kaiser Bautechnik; Kuehn Associates;**
Fischer Energie & Haustechnik; Amstein & Walthert;

Planungsgruppe Karnasch-Hackstein
Quantity Surveyors **Davis Langdon & Everest**
Büro am Lützowplatz
Lifts, Materials, Handling Technology **Jappsen & Stangler**
Cladding Consultants **Emmer Pfenninger & Partner**
Photography **Richard Davies**
Programme **1992, 1995–99 (construction)**

Future Systems

Hallfield School, London

The Hallfield Prototype is a new low-cost, modular, pre-fabricated, 60 sq.m double classroom building, circular in shape, naturally ventilated and represents the latest in design and construction methods. The planned erection of six of these double classrooms in the central London setting of an existing school designed by Denys Lasdun in 1951, now listed grade 2, marks an important addition to modern school design.

This modular classroom design will not only enhance the nursery, infant, junior and adult education activities of Hallfield School and its wider community, but also set an example to other schools up and down the country, showing how visionary architectural design can help restore a troubled education system to its rightful place at the centre of community life.

Each Hallfield Prototype will provide teachers, pupils and administrators with a flexible space that is not only of the highest design quality, but also possesses an unprecedentedly rapid relocation and reconfiguration capability that will enable it to be adjusted quickly to the widest range of school and community needs. The structure and external envelope of the classrooms will admit a high level of daylight coupled with high thermal efficiency and ultra-low energy consumption. The design will also feature large equipment storage spaces, and standards of administrative and service flexibility that are not often found in other schools.

This low-cost building is capable of being erected or dismantled within a six-week summer vacation; a building easily subdivided or opened out and one designed from the outset to accommodate the computers and information technology increasingly required in all school buildings. The relevance of these innovations to the needs of schools across the country, and the feasibility of producing large numbers of Hallfield Prototypes for wider use, have been embodied in the building's design.

Client **Hallfield School**

Architect **Future Systems**

Structural Engineer **Ove Arup & Partners**

Cost consultants **Hanscomb**

Environmental Engineer **Ove Arup & Partners**

Landscape Architects **Townshend Landscape Architects**

Photography **Richard Davies**

Hodder Associates

Centenary Building, University of Salford

The four-storey orthogonal building, with a three-storey, highly-glazed, free-form element facing the courtyard, is of crosswall construction. A series of flat roofs steps down from east to west. The orthogonal element defines the perimeter of the campus, while the counterpoint of the free-form element sits in a collegiate courtyard establishing a dialogue with the landscape.

The building provides three significantly different types of accommodation: cellular rooms for tutors extend the full length of the front of the building; a slightly wider span behind provides both flexible studios and seminar rooms; and the wider span of the free-form structure accommodates more inflexible CAD suites, lecture theatres and a huge top floor industrial design studio.

Between the two forms is a linear atrium 'street', the roof of which cantilevers from the west-facing building. This element does not touch the east-facing building, and the tension it creates is only relieved by the lightweight steel bridges. All horizontal circulation is via galleries overlooking this space, and on the first floor it is possible to cross the atrium void.

Client **University of Salford**

Architect **Hodder Associates**

Structural Engineer **SMP Atelier One**

Quantity Surveyor **Appleyard & Trew**

Building Services Engineer **Miller Walmsley Partnership**

Management Contractor **AMEC Design & Management Ltd.**

Photography **Dennis Gilbert**

Cost **£4m**

Programme **1993–95**

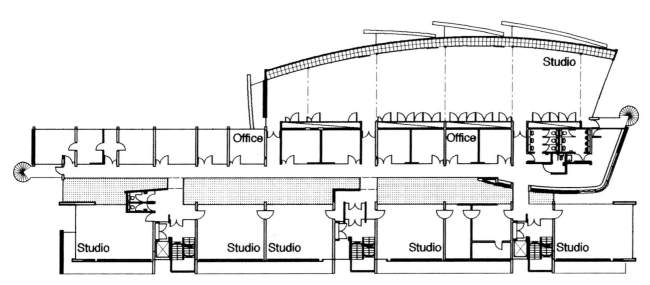

Michael Hopkins and Partners

The New Parliamentary Building, London

The main purpose of the building is to provide offices for 210 Members of Parliament, but it will also accommodate a library, catering facilities and a suite of committee rooms. The basic form of the building is very simple – a six-storey rectangular block with a central courtyard. The entrance hall gives direct access, via a grand staircase, to the committee rooms on the first floor. The courtyard is surrounded at ground- and first-floor levels by cloister-like corridors.

At second-floor level, the courtyard is covered with a vaulted glass roof creating a landscaped conservatory with a bar, a cafeteria and a library reading area. Members' offices are located on the upper five floors; committee rooms, conference facilities and the Clerk's Department are on the first floor; restaurants, shops and common facilities are on the ground floor.

Inside the building, the construction materials have been used to their maximum advantage in the design of the energy-efficient heating and cooling systems. The optimum use of natural light reduces the need for artificial lighting and saves energy costs.

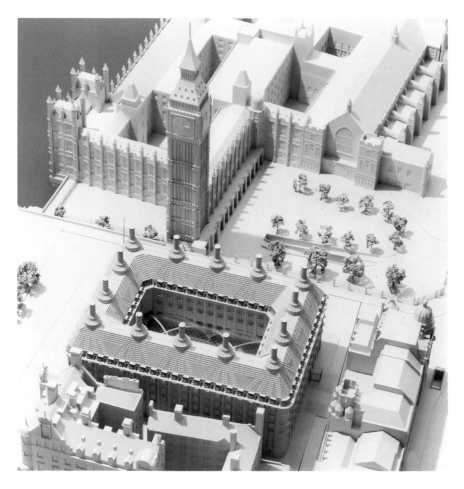

Client **House of Commons Accommodation and Works Committee Parliamentary Works Directorate**

Architect **Michael Hopkins and Partners**

Project Management **TBV Consult**

Structural Engineer **Ove Arup & Partners**

Quantity Surveyor **Gardiner & Theobald**

Construction Management **Laing Management Ltd**

Acoustics Consultant **Arup Acoustics**

Photography **Richard Davies**

Programme **1995–**

Michael Hopkins and Partners

University of Nottingham Campus Masterplan, Nottingham

Situated within a mile of the existing main campus at University Park, the new campus will be constructed on a former industrial site which will be completely regenerated. The linear urban site contains severe and apparently conflicting constraints: to the north-east there is the massive presence of bonded warehousing; to the west a suburban housing estate.

To provide a buffer between the existing housing estate and the new buildings, a lake has been created, along which a lakeside promenade provides access to the major buildings. A resource centre is sited on an island within the lake and axially related to a central teaching facility. Flanking both sides are the lakeside teaching departments with the student residences situated on the site periphery.

The masterplan features two entrances to the site, both of which employ a formal avenue as a prelude to the campus proper, evoking the City of Nottingham's famous boulevards.

Client **The University of Nottingham**

Client Project Manager **Turner & Townsend Project Management**

Architect **Michael Hopkins and Partners**

Structural and Services Engineer **Ove Arup & Partners**

Environmental Engineer **Battle McCarthy**

Construction Engineer **Bovis Construction**

Acoustic Consultant **Arup Acoustics**

Photography **Richard Davies**

Programme **1995–**

Ian Ritchie Architects

Glass Reception Hall, International Exhibition Centre, Leipzig

At 79m wide, 237m long and 28m high, the glass hall is the largest single-volume glass building of the 20th century. It provides reception, relaxation and meeting areas for visitors and seven glass bridges which connect these winter-gardens to the trade exhibition and conference halls. The vaulted structure is composed of an external, orthogonal, single-layer grid shell spanning 80m, of uniform tube diametre and stiffened by primary arches at 25m centres. The envelope is composed of low-iron, laminated, toughened glass panels suspended from the grid shell and includes discreet ventilation and smoke extract openings. Glass louvres run the full length of the hall on both sides at low level. They are opened by means of electric motor-driven torque tubes, which are connected to the glass sheets by profile cut stainless steel arms. Specially designed neoprene extrusions between overlapping sheets provide a safe as well as waterproof seal. The bridges are independent steel structures enclosed with curved, toughened-glass sheets. A large percentage of them open in a similar way to the glass louvres to provide natural ventilation. Lighting is integrated into the handrails.

Client **Leipzig Neue Messe/Von Gerkan Marg + Partner**
Glass Hall Architects **Von Gerkan Marg + Partner**
in collaboration with Ian Ritchie Architects
Glass Engineering **Ian Ritchie Architects**
Structural Concept **Ian Ritchie Architects**
assisted by Ove Arup & Partners
Structural Engineer **Ingenieurbüro Polonyl & Partners, Cologne**
Services Engineer **HL Technik AG, Munich**
Quantity Surveyor **GMP assisted by Ian Ritchie Architects**
Project Managers **Rauch & Wiese**
Contractor **ARGE Mero-Seele**
Landscape Consultant **Wehberg Lange Eppinger Schmidtke**
Photography **Jocelyn van den Bossche**
Cost **£25m**
Programme **1993–95**

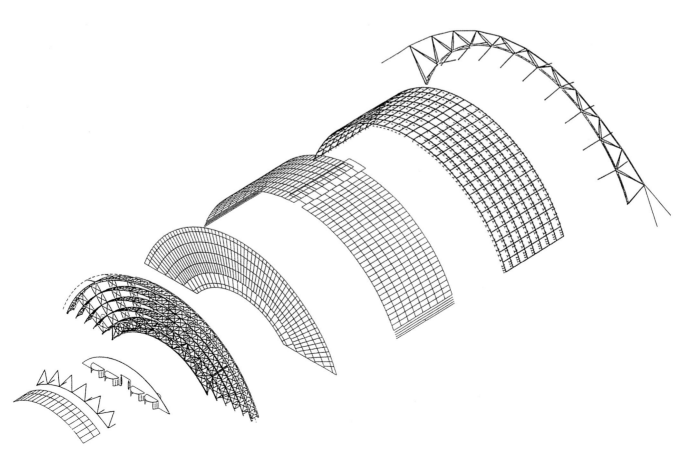

Michael Wilford and Partners

British Embassy, Berlin

The British Embassy will re-occupy its central location on Wilhelmstrasse when the German Federal Government moves back to the reinstated capital of Germany. The nearby Berlin Wall sterilised the immediate area for thirty years, and only now is there the opportunity for the district to regain something of its earlier twentieth-century pre-eminence.

The street facade establishes a 22m-high stone plane across the full width of the site, as specified by the city's urban development guidelines. This plane is an expression of the layered internal organisation of the building, comprising base, ceremonial and office levels. An abstract collage of forms is revealed through an opening in the facade, marking the entrance and registering the special character of the Embassy in relation to the neutrality of adjacent buildings.

The entrance court provides an elegant set-down within the building and is a transition in ambience and culture between the city and the Embassy. An oak tree at its centre will provide an immediate association with Britain. On ceremonial occasions visitors will be escorted up the grand staircase to the winter-garden on the *piano nobile* which, with its circular rooflights and generous windows overlooking the entrance court, forms the internal focus of the Embassy.

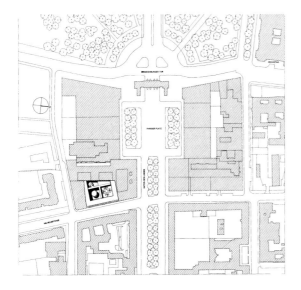

Client **Overseas Estates Department**
Architect **Michael Wilford and Partners**
Project Manager **Schal International, London**
Structural, Mechanical and Electrical Engineers **Whitby & Bird, London**
Quantity Surveyor **Hanscomb, London**
Building Physicist **Dr. Flohrer, Berlin**
Fire Consultant **Hosser Hass & Partner, Berlin-Grunewald**
Photography **Chris Edgecombe**
Programme **1995–99**

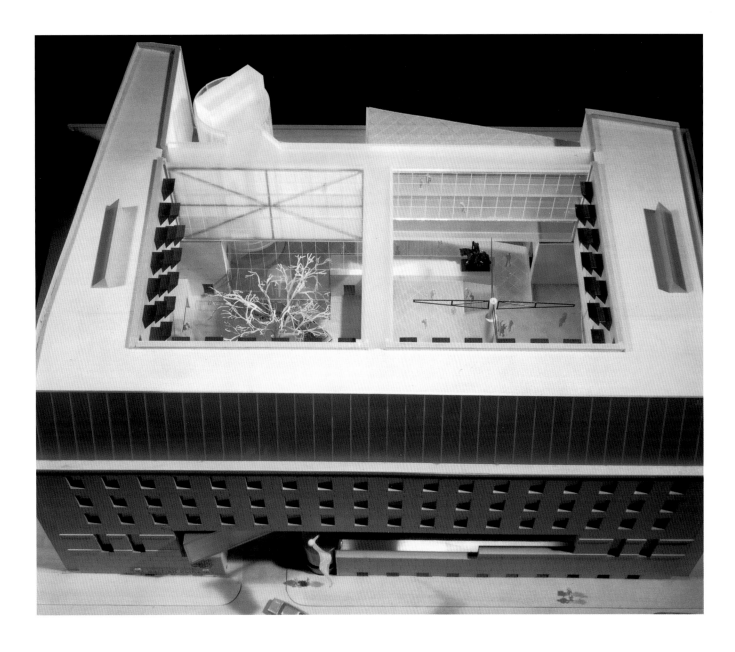

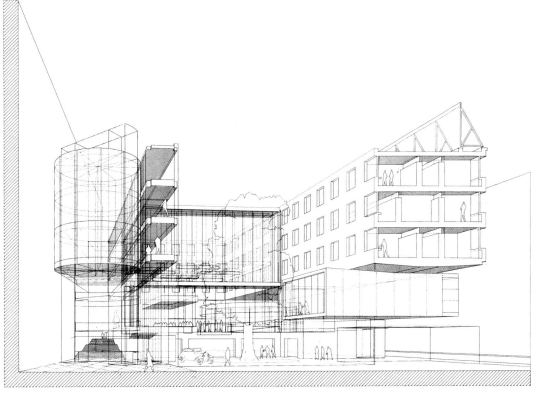

Alsop and Störmer Architects
North Greenwich Station, London

Nick Derbyshire Design Associates
International Terminal, Ashford

Terry Farrell and Partners
Inchon International Airport Transportation
Centre, Seoul, Korea

Foster and Partners
Canary Wharf Station, London

Foster and Partners
Millennium Bridge, London

Future Systems
Floating Bridge, West India Quay, London

Nicholas Grimshaw and Partners
Pusan High Speed Rail Complex, South Korea

Nicholas Grimshaw and Partners
Expansion of Zurich Airport

Nicholas Grimshaw and Partners
Waterloo International Terminal, London

Lifschutz Davidson
Royal Victoria Dock Bridge, London

Ian Ritchie Architects
Bermondsey Underground Station, London

Richard Rogers Partnership
Terminal 5, Heathrow, London

Michael Wilford and Partners
Abando Interchange, Bilbao

Chris Wilkinson Architects
& Jan Bobrowski and Partners
South Quay Footbridge, South Dock, London

Chris Wilkinson Architects
Stratford Market Depot, London

Chris Wilkinson Architects
Stratford Station, London

Transport

British architecture is at its best when celebrating movement and travel. Some of the country's greatest structures are railway and underground stations, and – more recently – airports. This, in part, reflects a very British fascination with model trains, cars and aeroplanes and a profound enjoyment of pure functional expression. When railways were introduced to congested Victorian cities in the mid-19th century, the station replaced the cathedral as the great civic monument of the age. Vast, elegant and economical glass and iron structures not only provided protection from the weather but also celebrated the theatre of travel, the drama of arrival and departure for the everyday passenger. Still today, one hundred years after their construction, three of London's Victorian railway stations – King's Cross, St Pancras and Victoria – remain shining examples of design excellence, a pure synthesis of architecture and engineering.

This tradition has been effortlessly extended to the new generation of transport buildings being realised in Britain today. Not unsurprisingly, it is the inheritor of the great Victorian engineering tradition – the high-tech school – that has found its natural expression in the new buildings of transport and communication. Like Norman Foster's Stansted Airport, many of the airport and railway buildings are a celebration of efficiency and light. Nicholas Grimshaw's enjoyment of detailing and anthropomorphism inspire his designs for Zurich airport and Waterloo Station in London with highly expressive forms that act as landmarks in the city fabric. Michael Wilford's transport interchange in Bilbao belongs to a more grounded, urban tradition that seeks to engage with the surrounding pattern of streets and public spaces, an approach reminiscent of Rafael Moneo's solid design for the San Pablo airport in Seville.

As Europe enters a new age of integration and global competitiveness, significant investment has been made in international and national transport infrastructure. A sophisticated high-speed rail system now connects many areas of central and northern Europe to Britain (through the Channel Tunnel). This infrastructure has given rise to a new generation of buildings – railway stations, transport interchanges and airports – that have an incisive presence in the European city. The traditional French town of Lille, for example, has reinvented itself as 'Euralille', a major commercial and business centre at the crossroads of European high-speed rail links. Retail, offices and conference centres are placed above and around a new station that connects Paris, Brussels and London in less than three hours.

These new transport structures have rekindled an interest in the art of travel, contributing to the emergence of a distinct typology with clear architectural connotations. The Jubilee Line Extension in London is a metropolitan example of this regional trend. The £2 billion project comprising 16 km of new tunnels, eleven new stations and a rail depot, is an innovative commissioning programme that will upgrade London's pioneering but ageing underground system. Each station is designed by a different architect – Alsop & Störmer, Norman Foster, Ian Ritchie and Chris Wilkinson are featured here – in order to provide variety of experience for the passenger. In their own way, each design is an ingenious exercise in bringing daylight as far down into the earth as possible. Clarity of movement and sense of orientation are the generators of an eclectic design aesthetic that marks a search for diversity and identity: a model for the transport environment of the future.

Alsop and Störmer Architects

North Greenwich Station, London

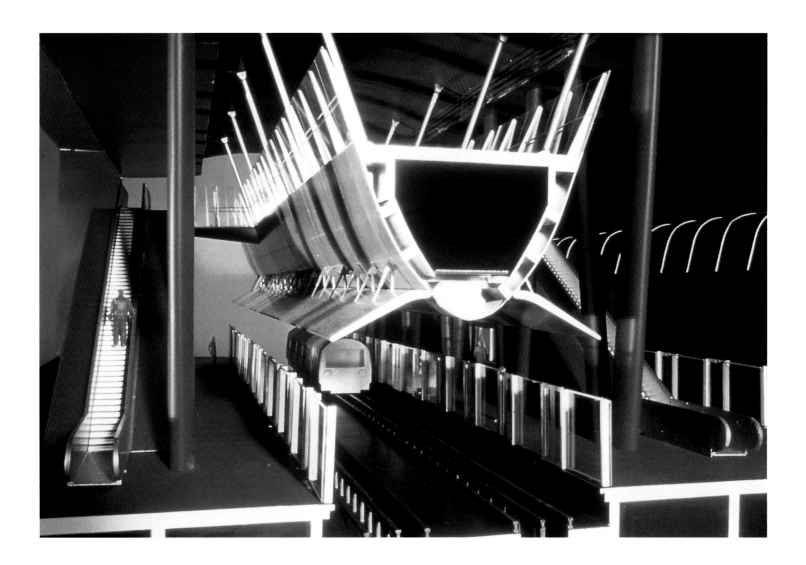

This is one of twelve new Underground stations that will form the extension to the Jubilee Line. The design comprises a series of objects within the shell, ensuring a simple logical sequence of movements into and away from the public areas.

The public areas comprise both island and side platforms. The ticket office, at a higher level towards the west, leads down to a dramatically shaped passenger concourse that is suspended from the concrete roof structure. Glass side panels provide the passenger with a view of the platforms, maintaining the feeling of volume and space. All the services are laid along the hollow core of the suspended concourse. The air handling ducts are also suspended within bright metallic extrusions.

The grand scale and simple elegance of this structure are enhanced by the use of ultramarine blue on the walls, floor and ceiling. The concourse, air ducts and escalators are all clad with bright stainless steel extrusions, and suspended within the ultramarine void.

Client **London Underground Limited**
Architects **Alsop & Störmer Architects**
Project Manager **Jubilee Line Extension Project Team**
Structural and Civil Engineers **Robert Benaim & Associates**
Environmental Engineers **Jubilee Line Extension Project Team**
Quantity Surveyor **Turner Fletcher Mills**
Lighting Engineers **Lighting Design Partnership**
Acoustic Engineers **Paul Gilveron**
Photography **Rodney Coyne**
Cost **£ 20m**
Programme **Currently on site completion: Spring 1998**

Nick Derbyshire Design Associates

International Terminal, Ashford

This is the second international station to be built in Britain following the completion of the Channel Tunnel; the first, at Waterloo, is grafted onto the existing station and is a terminus. In contrast, Ashford is a through station and required the rebuilding of the existing domestic station as well as the new station for international trains.

Steel and glass are materials frequently found in railway architecture. The principle adopted in this design approach is that the supports should express themselves in mass and colour, while the infill or skin should be subservient within the structure. The external skin is diaphanous, allowing natural light in during the day and artificial light out at night. At roof level, an elliptical service pod forms a spine to the roof structure, terminating in two 'book-end' plant rooms. The curved ends of the building have both been detailed to incorporate curved steelwork, aluminium aerofoil edges and an infill of translucent glass blocks. The glass blocks are used primarily for their quality of light, as well as providing security to the customs areas. Both ends are topped with a circular lantern, again in glass blocks which allow natural light to penetrate into the non-public core stairs and which act as beacons at night.

Client **Railtrack plc**

Architect **Nick Derbyshire Design Associates Ltd.**

Structural Engineer **WSP Group**

M&E Services Engineer **DSSR**

Quantity Surveyor **Gardiner & Theobald**

Private Finance Initiative Contractor **Laing Civil Engineering**

Photography **Paul Childs**

Cost **£100m**

Programme **1993–95**

Terry Farrell and Partners

Inchon International Airport Transportation Centre, Seoul, Korea

The integrated transportation centre for the New Seoul International Airport is currently under construction. The scheme is now at the detailed design stage and the design is in the tradition of the great transportation concourses with clear spans of 180 metres and a vaulted roof over 40 metres high. The building integrates two high-speed and two standard rail systems, approximately 5,000 car-parking spaces and an inter-terminal passenger movement system. When completed the new transportation system will eventually cater for 60 million passengers annually.

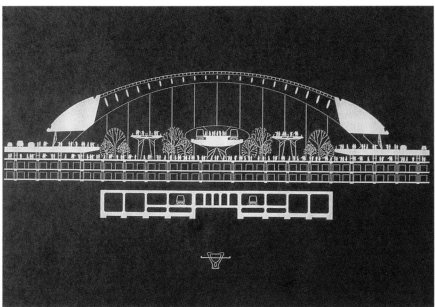

Client **KOACA (Korea Airport Construction Authority)**
Architect **Terry Farrell and Partners and**
Samoo Architects & Engineers
Structural Engineer **Daniel, Mann, Johnson & Mendenhall**
Quanitity Surveyor **Samoo Architects & Engineers**
M&E Services Engineer **Samoo Architects & Engineers**
Civil Engineer **Samoo Architects & Engineers and DMJM**
CAD Image **Terry Farrell and Partners**
Models **Terry Farrell and Partners**
Photography **Terry Farrell and Partners**
Cost **US $ 300m**
Programme **Completion: End 2000**

Foster and Partners

Canary Wharf Station, London

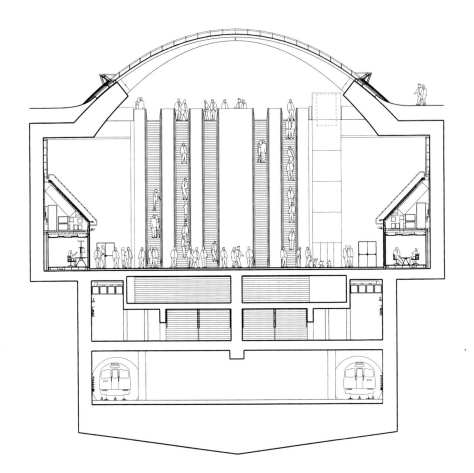

Canary Wharf Station is the largest on the new extension to the Jubilee Line. The design seeks to minimise the physical and visual impact of above ground station structures by creating a park above it.

Two main passenger entrances are provided. Both enclosures take the form of large glass-domed bubbles, glowing with light at night time. Each spans 20m and is carefully integrated into the sloping grass banks at either end of the main station park, to be Canary Wharf's principal public recreation space. There is a third smaller entrance at the eastern side of Canary Wharf to accommodate growth.

The 250m-long station is of cut and cover construction, built within a reclaimed dock. Twenty escalators descend from the entrance canopies down to platform level. The ticket hall will be located within the station cavern together with shops, London Underground offices and public amenities. The entire cavern will be clad in glass. Platform edge doors have also been designed for this and all other stations on the new line.

Client **London Underground Limited**
Architect **Foster and Partners**
Civil Engineer **Posford Duvivier**
Project Management and Engineering **Jubilee Line**
Extension Team Project
Structural Engineers **Ove Arup & Partners**
Lighting **Claude Engle**
Quantity Surveyor **Davis Langdon & Everest**
Photography **Nigel Young**
Programme **1994–98**

Foster and Partners

Millennium Bridge, London

The new Millennium Bridge will be London's first new river crossing for over 100 years and the capital's first pedestrian bridge. It will link two of the capital's most significant public spaces and buildings – St Paul's Cathedral to the north and the area around the new Tate Gallery of Modern Art, and the Globe Theatre to the south – creating a new route between the north and south banks of the river. Undisturbed by vehicles and city noise, it will also be a striking new architectural landmark in its own right, opening up unique new views of London, in particular of St Paul's Cathedral. The bridge will be completed in time for the millennium.

Client **Millenium Bridge Trust**
Architect **Foster and Partners**
Sculptor **Sir Anthony Caro**
Structural Engineer **Ove Arup & Partners**
Quantity Surveyor **Davis Langdon & Everest**
Lighting **Claude Engle**
Wind Analysis **Rowan, Williams, Davis and Irwin**
Construction Advisors **Schal International**
Photography **Hayes Davidson (montage)**
Programme **1997–2000**

Future Systems

Floating Bridge, West India Quay, London

The bridge links two very important areas of very different scales – the large commercial development of Canary Wharf and the smaller scale of the 19th-century warehouses on West India Quay – providing a new urban link to promote dockside events, cafés and exhibitions along the waterfront.

The concept of the pontoon bridge has been known since 2000 BC, and this design reinterprets that ancient tradition creating a gently-arched structure floating on four pairs of pontoons. The plan form tapers towards the centre increasing the sense of perspective and the lightness of the structure. The deck is gently ramped in two sections joined by a central opening section which is lifted hydraulically with a simple, balanced cantilever action allowing boats to pass. The decking is aluminium while the main body of the bridge is mild steel. At night, stainless steel handrails with integral lighting illuminate the bridge decking, emphasising its floating quality and softly-curved plan.

Client **London Docklands Development Corporation**
Architect **Future Systems**
Structural Engineer **Anthony Hunt Associates**
Mechanical Engineer **Rendel Palmer & Tritton**
Lighting Consultant **Lighting Design Partnership**
Quantity Surveyor **Bucknall Austin**
Main Contractor **Littlehampton Welding**
Photography **Richard Davies**
Cost **£1.7m**
Programme **January–August 1996**

Nicholas Grimshaw and Partners

Pusan High Speed Rail Complex, South Korea

The masterplan proposal is for a two-kilometre stretch of existing railway land adjoining Pusan Harbour and a 16-platform station. The site is treated as an 'edge' which mediates between the mountain and existing street pattern on one side, and the sea on the other – a key position in the natural amphitheatre of Pusan Bay.

Existing streets cross the railway via a transfer deck supporting new buildings, arranged to form an asymmetrical section. Lower levels are protected from high winds by a 'green beach' formed from continuous, sloping grass roofs. Behind lies a two-kilometre-long 'green canyon' which will enjoy a similar microclimate to that on the landside beach sand-dunes, only here the dunes are hollow and full of commercial facilities. Along this deck runs a new pedestrian axis; this is the thoroughfare at the heart of the scheme.

Taller buildings are expressed as a series of independent organic forms which appear to float above the landscaping; the station is just one such object along this procession. Although its elliptical form is derived from the concourse plan below, which works as a hub, the resulting tilted and domed honeycomb structure provides a new landmark for the city – the Eye of Pusan Bay.

Client **Korean Highspeed Rail Company**
Architects **Nicholas Grimshaw and Partners and Kunwon Architects**
Structural Engineer **Ove Arup & Partners**
M&E Services Engineer **Ove Arup & Partners**
Cost **£240m**
Photography Image **Nicholas Grimshaw and Partners**
Programme **1997–2002**

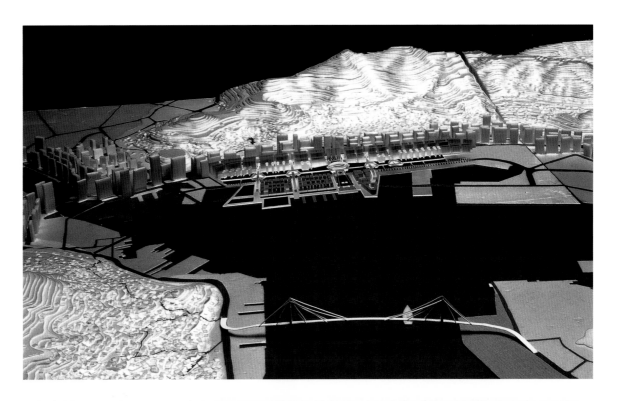

Nicholas Grimshaw and Partners

Expansion of Zurich Airport

The proposal covers three main areas: the landside centre, the airside centre and Parkhaus C. The landside centre, situated above the mainline train station, and Parkhaus C are both designed to improve the efficiency of the airport's check-in facility by providing sixty new check-in desks. Passenger flows to and from the main terminal buildings will be improved through the provision of a single clear direction of traffic for the departing passengers and a new direct connection to the arrivals hall.

The airside centre will expand and improve existing retail facilities, with extra catering and lounge areas to maximise commercial income. The principal architectural and psychological motive of the airside centre is to create a strong sense of place. This is achieved through the use of a unifying sweeping roofscape, itself a direct response to the plan form, providing a dynamic environment and image for Zurich Airport.

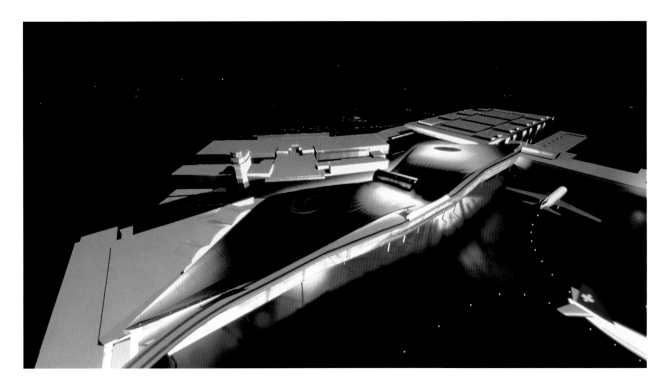

Client **Flughafen Immobilien Gesellschaft (FIG)**
Architect **Nicholas Grimshaw and Partners**
Associate Architects **I & B, Itten & Brechbuhl AG**
Structural/M&E Engineer **Ernst Basler & Partners**
Consultant Engineer **Ove Arup & Partners**
Quantity Surveyor **Perolini Baumanagement**

Retail Consultant **John Herbert Partnership**
Cost **£162m**
Photography Image **Nicholas Grimshaw and Partners,
Michael Dyer Associates**
Programme **1996–2002**

Nicholas Grimshaw and Partners

Waterloo International Terminal, London

The building is designed as a clear-span steel structure in the spirit of the new railway age. The roof and cladding are constructed of glass and matte-finish stainless steel, which ensure low maintenance and long life for the building envelope.

The roof is a three-pinned arch, with the 'centre pin' located to one side to create an asymmetrical geometry that meets the requirements of internal train clearances within the tight constraints of the raised viaduct structure. The structure is essentially a bow-string arch with the cable reversing from inside to outside at the point of contra-flexure to create an articulate and legible structure to the western elevation.

Each passenger-handling zone services a platform with a people conveyor, an escalator (both reversible) and a lift. Arriving passengers flow downwards from the platform level to collect baggage and clear customs and immigration control before entering the new double-height concourse containing shops and restaurants, as well as business facilities such as computers and fax machines.

Client **British Railway Board**

Architect **Nicholas Grimshaw and Partners**

Structural Engineer **YRM, Anthony Hunt Associates, Cass Hayward & Partners with Tony Gee & Partners, British Rail Network Civil Engineer, Sir Alexander Gibb & Partners**

M&E Services Engineer **J. Roger Preston & Partners**

Quantity Surveyor **Davis Langdon & Everest**

Construction Manager **Bovis Contruction Ltd.**

Planning Consultant **Montague Evans**

Fire Consultant **Ove Arup & Partners**

Lighting Consultant **Lighting Design Partnership**

Signage Consultant **Henrion Ludlow Schmidt**

Flow Planning Consultant **Sir Alexander Gibb & Partners**

Photography **Peter Cook, Reid and Peck**

Programme **1990–93**

Lifschutz Davidson

Royal Victoria Dock Bridge, London

The new footbridge, which crosses the Royal Victoria Dock in a single span, is based on the century-old principle of the 'transporter bridge'. In its initial phase, the lightweight bridge deck, accessed from pairs of scenic lifts each end, will accommodate pedestrian traffic. A planned 'people-mover' cabin, suspended under the bridge and supervised by an operator, accommodating forty-five passengers, will not be installed right away, but the design will include the necessary track and infrastructure. Once installed, the people-mover will ferry passengers across the dock in a gentle arc, providing spectacular views.

No part of the bridge deck is less than 15m above water level and the bridge has a minimal cross-sectional area. Where the structure deepens, it extends above rather than below bridge deck level. This results in a series of distinctive 'humps' on the bridge deck which are reminiscent of the keels of upturned boats and can be used as vantage points to watch sailing events in the dock.

Client **London Docklands Development Corporation**
Architect **Lifschutz Davidson**
Engineer **Techniker Ltd**
M&E Design **Allott & Lomax**
Quantity Surveyor **Davis Langdon & Everest**
Lighting Design **Equation Lighting**
Photography Image **Lifschutz Davidson**
Cost **£4m**
Programme **1997—98**

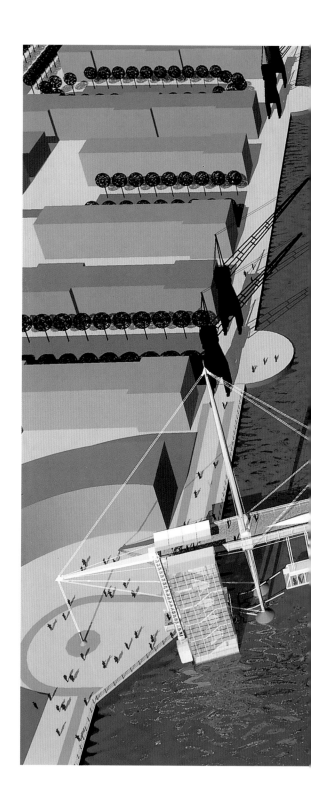

Ian Ritchie Architects

Bermondsey Underground Station, London

The treatment of the above ground structure and the internal fit-out of the public areas seeks to extend the construction hierarchy by the treatment of metal castings, stainless steel plate and floor finishes to achieve a visible tactile quality in the areas of immediate public contact.

At street level, the station roof emerges with a gentle curve, cantilevering over the main entrance and public footway forming a protective canopy. It is a translucent glazed structure which will transmit daylight into the building, some sunlight even reaching the platform area. This will create a visible drama of space and depth, alleviating the sense of tension and claustrophobia often associated with sub-surface environments. The roof is supported by simple linear beams wrapped in a perforated stainless steel skin. Acoustic material within the beams provides attenuation to the voids above platforms and escalators.

The perimeter of the building is predominantly transparent, allowing the public clear views into the station – an additional measure of security for passengers and staff. A continuous 'leaning pad' adjacent to the glazing will provide a further protective barrier for people walking along the street. The artificial lighting will enhance the night-time visual quality of the station interior. A continuous illuminated blue glass frieze and blue glass bench seat create a visual harmony between the station canopy at street level and the platform, and are the 'jewellery' of the station.

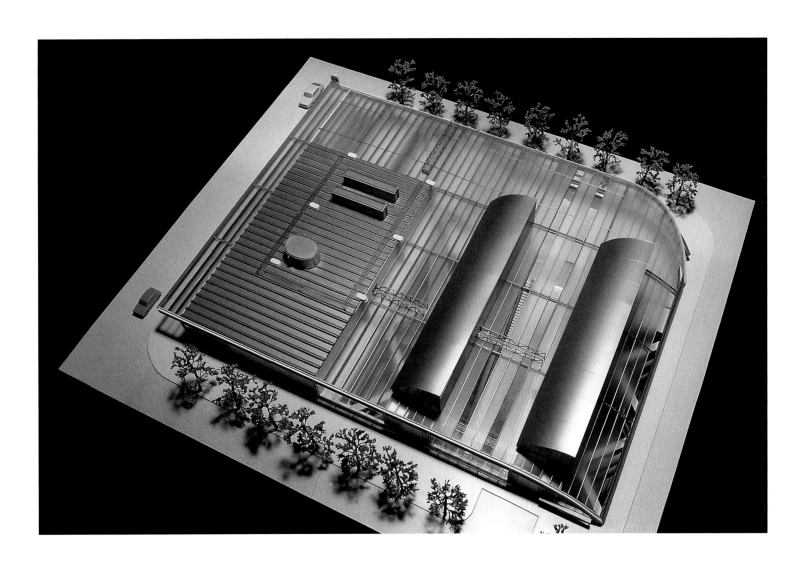

Client **London Underground Ltd.**

Architect **Ian Ritchie Architects**

Civil Engineer **Sir William Halcrow & Partners**

Additional structural engineering advice **Ove Arup & Partners**

Quantity Surveyor **Hanscomb Partnership**

Lighting Consultant **Lighting Design Vienna**

Acoustic Consultant **Paul Gillieron**

Landscape Consultant **Charlie Funke Associates**

Photography **Jocelyne van den Bossche**

Cost **£ 24m**

Programme **Completion: Spring 1998**

Richard Rogers Partnership

Terminal 5, Heathrow Airport, London

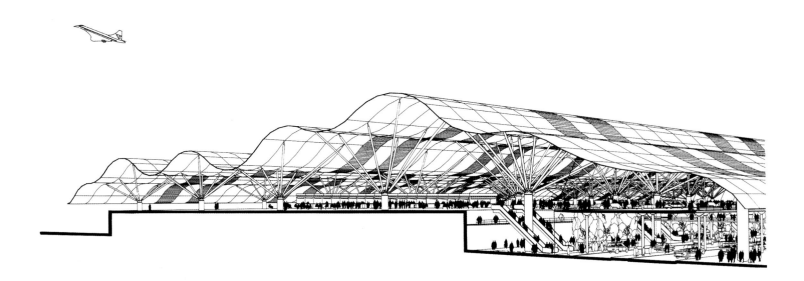

These strategic planning studies for the design of a new terminal include hotel and airport support facilities, passenger and cargo terminals to be built in phases – the first phase to be opened in 2002 and fully completed in 2016. The terminal and satellites will be used primarily by British Airways for both domestic and international routes and are perceived as a gateway to UK and Europe.

The core processing terminal with remote satellites linked by people-movers will be vertically linked, segregated with Departures above Arrivals and with a technical zone below. The layout is split north/south to accommodate phasing and a separation of modes of travel. All the public transportation systems are below ground. The roof design will be undulating and large-span allowing maximum flexibility, visibility and easy passenger flow and providing a fifth elevation when viewed from the air. There is a minimal number of vertical structures which are supported in as elegant a way as possible. It is highly flexible inside – currently a single-storey airport, although this may change.

Client **British Airport Authority**
Architect **Richard Rogers and Partnership**
Structural Engineer **Ove Arup & Partners**
Sub-Structure Engineer **J. Roger Preston & Partners; DSSR**
Quantity Surveyor **Turner & Townsend, MDA,**
Davis Langdon & Everest
Management Contractor **Bovis**
Photography **Eamon O'Mahony**
Cost **£400m**
Programme **1989–2002, 2016 (fully completed)**

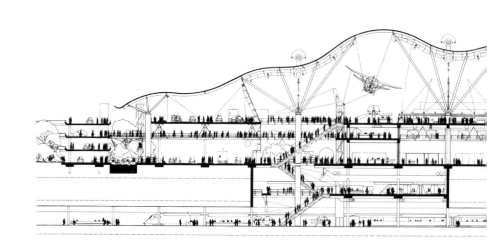

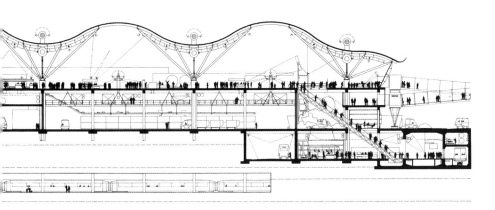

Michael Wilford and Partners

Abando Interchange, Bilbao

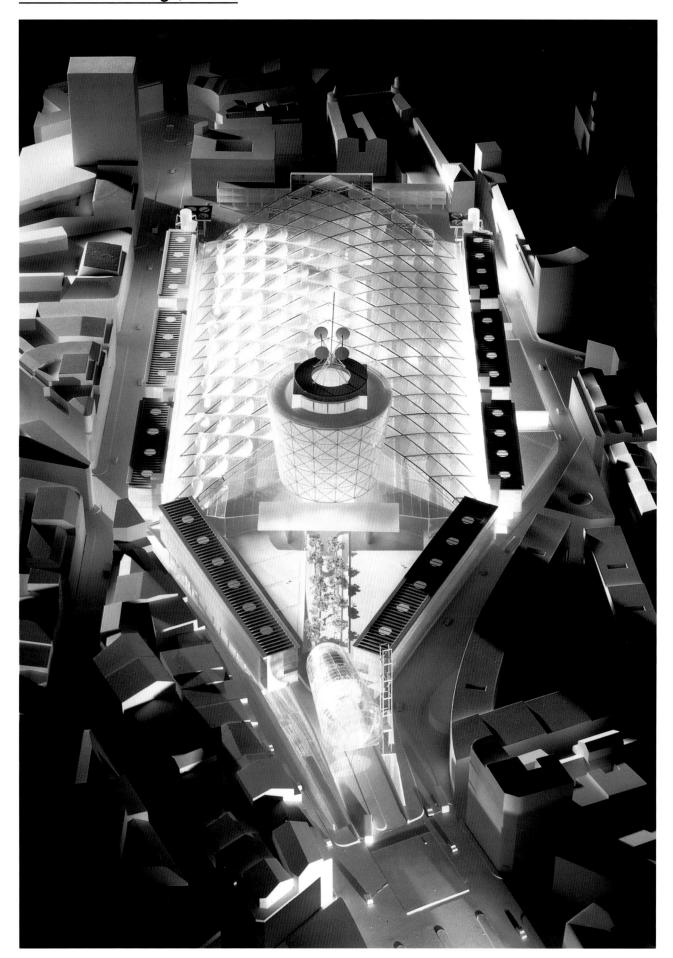

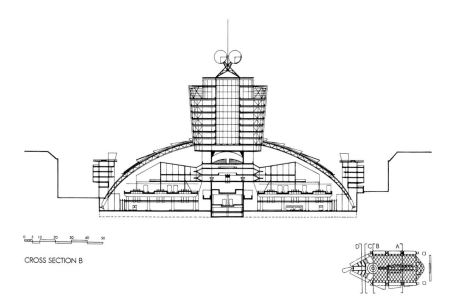

CROSS SECTION B

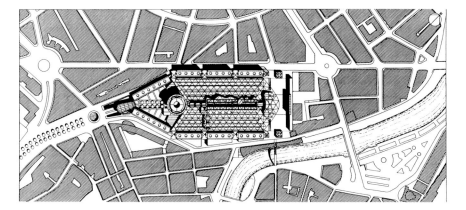

The new Abando Interchange will forge strong connections between the medieval and 19th-century quarters of the city and assist revitalisation of the central area. It will incorporate existing disparate bus and train passenger termini into one central facility, which is linked to the Metro and adjacent streets, to provide convenient access and interconnection between all modes of public transport. It also contains a retail concourse, World Trade Centre, post office, offices, hotel and housing and includes plans for the construction of a new public plaza.

The new plaza is the forecourt of the Interchange and forms a new centre of social activity and orientation for visitors. The dramatic vaulted roof of the Interchange will register its presence on the city skyline. Trains will emerge from a tunnel into the grand station hall, which is flooded with daylight from the vaulted roof above, providing a dramatic entry into the city.

Client **Estación Intermodal de Abando**
Architect **Michael Wilford & Partners Ltd.**
Associate Architects **Deurbe SA**
Structural Engineer **Ove Arup & Partners**
Cost Consultant **Davis Langdon Edetco SA**
Cladding Consultant **Atelier One & Arup Facade Engineering**
Photography **Chris Edgecombe**
Programme **1992–2003**

Chris Wilkinson Architects & Jan Bobrowski and Partners

South Quay Footbridge, South Dock, London

The design of this 180m cable-stayed bridge features two raking masts and a sinuous deck curved in both plan and elevation. The 'S'-shaped bridge comprises two identical halves, each one cable-supported from a tall raking mast. One half is static, while the other swings open about its mast to allow boats to pass.

The 32m-high masts support an array of stay cables connecting to a cylindrical spine beam from which the steel deck structure is cantilevered. A deck of grooved European oak planks is laid over the structure. To one side of the timber deck a raking steel balustrade supports an aluminium handrail incorporating continuous linear lighting. To the other side a curved, perforated stainless steel screen acts as a man-made hedge to offer protection from prevailing winds.

The design is a combination of functionality and sculpted form in architectural engineering. Curved forms and slender proportions act in contrast to the bulk and uniformity of the surrounding buildings, with the kinetics of the design providing excitement for bridge users and observers alike.

Client **London Docklands Development Corporation**
Architect **Chris Wilkinson Architects Ltd.**
Engineer **Jan Bobrowski & Partners**
Quantity Surveyor **Bucknall Austin**
Contractors **Christiani Neilsen Ltd.**
Photography **Morley Von Sternberg**
Cost **£2.5m**
Programme **Opened to the public 20 May 1997**

Chris Wilkinson Architects

Stratford Market Depot, London

The 100m-wide arched roof covers eleven maintenance bays where entire trains will be cleaned, serviced and repaired. Specialist workshops and stores are located alongside with a separate office and amenity buildings connected by a glazed link. The traction substation completes the chain of ancillary buildings linked by a direct service road.

On the other side of the main shed, the circular, glazed control room is housed in a curvilinear building between tracks overlooking incoming lines and the adjacent trains' stabling yard.

The 30° 'diagrid' roof structure of the main shed is clad with a self-finished aluminium seamed roof on a continuous shallow curve with wide gutters at the sides for easy maintenance. Strip rooflights are located between seams of the roof to provide good natural light. The side walls are clad with horizontal profiled sheeting in a silver pvf2 finish, up to the underside of the overhanging roof structure, with clerestory glazing above. The north elevation is fully glazed above train door level with a purpose-designed suspended glass wall assembly and, on the south elevation, a translucent, insulated fibreglass panel system to provide good daylight without glare or heat build-up.

Client **London Underground Jubilee Line Extension Project**

Architect **Chris Wilkinson Architects Ltd.**

Quantity Surveyor, Civil and Structural Engineer

Hyder Consulting Ltd.

M&E Services Engineer **Hurley Palmer Partneship**

Environmental Consultant **Loren Butt Consultancies**

Photography **Dennis Gilbert/View**

Cost **approx. £18m**

Programme **On-site April 1994, buildings completed April 1996, project completion due mid-1998**

Chris Wilkinson Architects

Stratford Station, London

The strong identity of this railway station and interchange will provide a new landmark in the town centre, giving a revitalised focus to the transport interchange area and completing the redevelopment of this key part of Stratford.

The form of the building is a curved roof springing from the upper-level walkway, parallel with the main railway lines, which sweeps up to a high glazed wall facing the town centre. The lower part of the curved roof is exposed and glazed on the outside face to provide views through to the mainline platforms beyond. The ends of the building are glazed and there is a clear view through from the entrance in the Eastern Concourse across to the Western Concourse. Creation of a single major space serves to unify the disparate elements of the various train services.

The roof form allows natural lighting and provides solar energy-assisted ventilation via the deep void in the double-skin roof through which air is drawn by the 'stack effect' and exhausted at the highest point. The natural ventilation maintains air movement and summer temperatures at comfortable levels; it also provides smoke ventilation in the event of fire.

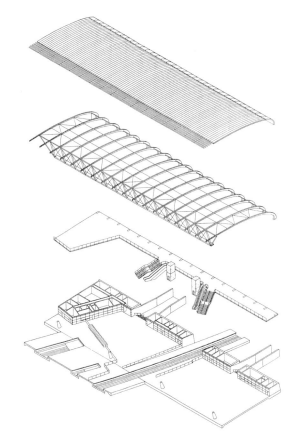

Client **London Underground Ltd Jubilee Line Extension Project Team & Stratford Development Partnership Limited**

Architect **Chris Wilkinson Architects Ltd.**

Structural Engineer/M&E Services Engineer **Hyder Consulting Ltd.**

Civil Engineer **Ove Arup & Partners**

Quantity Surveyor **Franklin & Andrews**

CAD Image **Hayes Davidson**

Models **Unit 22, 1:100 model; Dominic Bettison, 1:500 & 1:200 models**

Photography **Andrew Putler**

Cost **£16m**

Programme **Start on site May 1996, completion due March 1998**

Arup Associates
Stadium, Manchester

ECD Architects and Proctor Matthews Architects
Mile End Sports Centre, London

Terry Farrell and Partners
New National Aquarium, London

Foster and Partners
Wembley Stadium, London

Future Systems
Media Centre, Lord's Cricket Ground, London

David Marks Julia Barfield Architects
British Airways Millennium Wheel, London

Richard Rogers Partnership
Millennium Experience, Greenwich, London

Leisure

The pursuit of leisure often coincides with a conscious celebration of architectural expression. The overtly decorated but fun-loving Victorian waterfront piers – such as the famous Brighton Pier – are endemic to a particular aspect of British popular culture. The richly textured Edwardian theatres and grand movie houses of the 1930s – with their horizontal emphasis and neon signage – are more recent exponents of this highly expressive architectural tradition.

This tradition has been catapulted forward to the 21st century as a result of a fortunate combination of increased funding and the British rediscovery of the art of pleasure. The National Lottery, whose effects on the country's cultural landscape are described in a previous section, has spawned a wide range of sports and entertainment buildings that are being realised across Britain.

Arup Associates' highly articulated Manchester Stadium is an architectural statement of considerable symbolic content that will play a key role in the regeneration of the city's economy. Norman Foster's plans for the temple of English football, Wembley Stadium in London, envisages an entire sports city centred on a massive multi-functional stadium. Significantly, the dynamic new design incorporates Wembley's famous twin towers, the iconic image of national football history, reflecting the very British desire for change without rupturing with the past.

The synthesis of tradition and change could not be more poignant than at Lord's Cricket Ground, the heart of Britain's cricket heritage. Over the last decade, this profoundly conservative establishment has consistently promoted contemporary design by commissioning some of the country's most talented designers, including Michael Hopkins, Nicholas Grimshaw, David Morley, and – most recently – Future Systems. It is a city within a city. The juxtaposition of cricket 'whites' and the impeccable green wicket provides a permanent focal point framed by a series of architectural masterpieces,

each distinct and idiosyncratic, yet brought together by this blanket of tradition and uniformity. The Future Systems Media Centre is an organic steel structure that completes this sequence with a viewing platform built with the unique precision and advanced technology of Britain's boat-building industry.

The pleasure of expressing form and structure underlies many of the other projects in this section. Barfield Marks' Millennium Wheel, the largest moving Ferris wheel to be built this century, is a synthesis of architecture and engineering. Its impact on London's skyline comes directly from the structure of the wheel and the mechanism that generates its movement. The scale and simplicity of its construction will ensure that the Wheel will become, albeit temporarily, a landmark in London's ever-changing skyline.

Arup Associates

Stadium, Manchester

The competition brief was for an international standard stadium to host the Commonwealth Games for capacities of 60–80,000, with full post-Olympic use and a closing roof. A circular seating plan is combined with an oval arena to create dramatic elevations, the sweeping form of which moderates the bulk of the building. The high sides provide protection from prevailing winds and low sun angles while providing a concentration of seats and supporting accommodation; the low sides allow sun onto the grassed arena and give a human scale to the structure.

A generous landscaped circulation space surrounds the stadium and, as they arrive, spectators will be directed into zones defined by large round towers wrapped by open circulation ramps. The ramps will give startling views across the city, while the towers combine circulation with a mast-and-cable roof structure to create a visual order and enhance crowd comfort and safety.

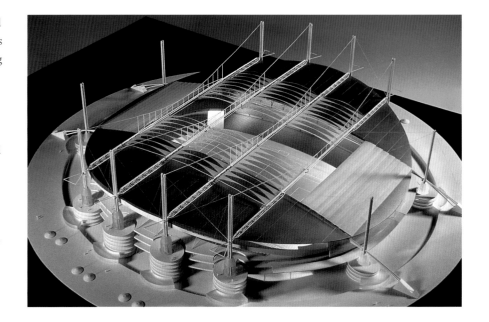

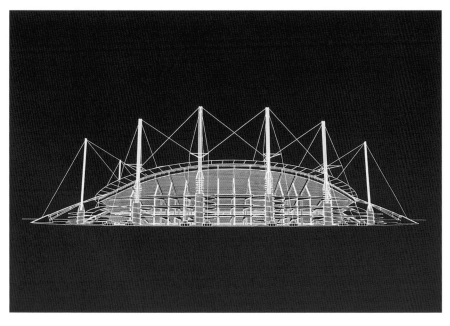

Client **Manchester City Council**
Architect, Structural Engineer and M&E Services Engineer
Arup Associates
CAD Image **Hayes Davidson**
Models **Millennium Models**
Photography **Andrew Putler**
Programme **1993 (design)**

ECD Architects and Proctor Matthews Architects

Mile End Sports Centre, London

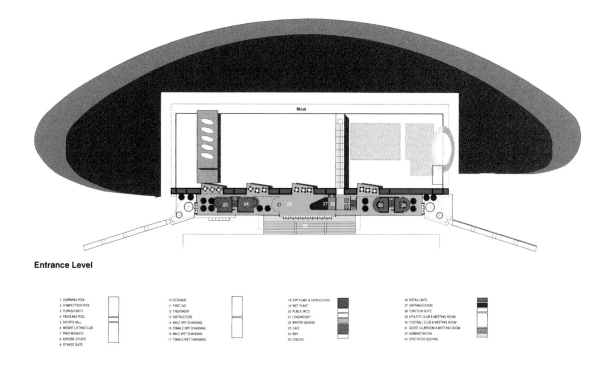

Moat

Entrance Level

1 LEARNING POOL	10 STORAGE	18 DRY PLANT & SERVICE VOID	26 RETAIL UNITS
2 COMPETITION POOL	11 FIRST AID	19 WET PLANT	27 ENTRANCE KIOSK
3 TURKISH BATH	12 TREATMENT	20 PUBLIC WC'S	28 FUNCTION SUITE
4 PADDLING POOL	13 INSTRUCTORS	21 LOADING BAY	29 ATHLETIC CLUB & MEETING ROOM
5 SPORTS HALL	14 MALE DRY CHANGING	22 WINTER GARDEN	30 FOOTBALL CLUB & MEETING ROOM
6 WEIGHT LIFTING CLUB	15 FEMALE DRY CHANGING	23 CAFE	31 GUEST CLUBROOM & MEETING ROOM
7 FREE WEIGHTS	16 MALE WET CHANGING	24 BAR	32 ADMINISTRATION
8 AEROBIC STUDIO	17 FEMALE WET CHANGING	25 CRECHE	33 SPECTATOR SEATING
9 FITNESS SUITE			

In response to the sensitive nature of the site, the building is partially sunk below ground level and covered with a grass mound. From the adjoining main road, the building is virtually indistinguishable from the landscape. From within the park, however, it is characterised by a glazed winter-garden which runs along its length. This is conceived as an 'incident' in the park, a 'sports' street which allows viewing of sporting activities, both internally and externally, on track and field.

The design, which accommodates a twelve-court multipurpose sports hall, a 25m eight-lane competition pool, a training pool and associated changing facilities, as well as sports shops and recreational space, is based on an energy and environmental strategy aimed at minimising running costs and environmental impact. The building envelope is highly insulated and roof-lights provide good, even natural daylighting. Ventilation is provided by natural and fan-assisted means, depending on seasonal and internal conditions.

Client **London Borough of Tower Hamlets**
Architect **ECD Architects and Proctor Matthews Architects**
Structural Engineer **Buro Happold**
M&E Services Engineer **Max Fordham & Partners**
Quantity Surveyor **Davis Langdon & Everest**
Landscape Design **London Borough of Tower Hamlets**
Photography Images **ECD Architects**
Cost **£14m**
Programme **1998–2000**

Terry Farrell and Partners

New National Aquarium, London

The concept for the new National Aquarium building is a powerful metaphor for a "core sample" of the earth's habitat. The natural habitat forms a microcosm, bringing together the elements of earth, water and air, combined with various forms of vegetation. The building's base is formed like geological strata, with natural rocks and metals shown in layers with fissures forming the main building element. Above, the cloud-like roof reacts to moderate the climate below. Acting as a solar collector and sunlight filter it also adjusts to naturally ventilate the spaces below. In winter, transparent blankets of insulation reduce heat loss and energy will be conserved throughout the year by carefully balancing and recovering the building's energy.

Organisationally, the building is arranged in four parts, each reflecting four representative world habitats. Two of these, in the middle, have natural daylight for the predominantly freshwater display for the UK habitat at the lowest level, and for the Indian one above. The two blank ends are clearly evident on the north and south side and contain the highly conditioned tropical/subtropical areas of the Red Sea and South Pacific habitats. The site layout responds to limits defined by the Victoria Dock. The building is located at one extreme end of the site and, as such, occupies a peninsula, with deep water on three sides. Visitors will enter the building by bridges and pathways over the watercourses and ponds of the UK exhibit, so that – on approaching – the building will give the appearance of being on an island.

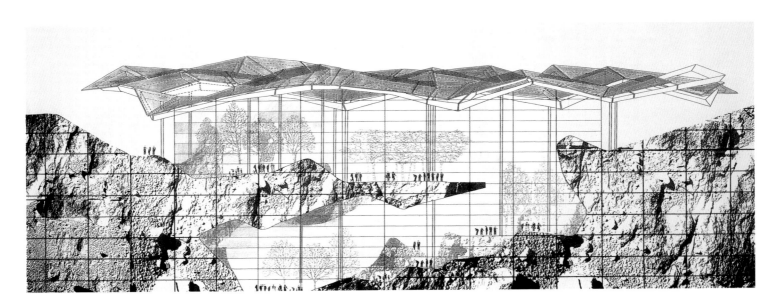

Client **Zoological Society of London/Kajima International Inc.**
Architect **Terry Farrell and Partners in association with**
Esherick, Homesy, Dodge & Davis
Structural Engineer and Services Engineer **Ove Arup & Partners**
Exhibition Consultants **Joseph A. Wetzel Associates Inc.**
Models **Terry Farrell and Partners**
Photography **Andrew Putler**
Cost **£54m**
Programme **Completion: Easter 2000**

Foster and Partners

Wembley Stadium, London

The design for a new national stadium at Wembley makes a special feature of the famous twin towers which will form an impressive gateway. Repositioning the towers has created extra space to allow the stadium to be spun round 90° with a new north-south axis; this reduces the sun's glare for players and improves spectator circulation. The shape of the seating bowl incorporates the idea of the 'Wembley Wave', creating a sweeping curve, flowing along the eastern and western sides, as the upper tier follows the external wall line. A retractable seating system will bring spectators close to the pitch, with improved sightlines and leg-room.

The external skin will act as a giant projection screen to provide a wall of moving images for spectators in the new square outside. The roof covers the entire stadium and has retractable panels which move to leave an opening extending beyond the playing areas. Translucent material ensures that natural daylight extends through-out the stadium.

Client **English National Stadium Trust**
Architect **Foster and Partners**
Stadium Architects **Atherden Fuller**
Structural Engineer **Ove Arup & Partners;**
Sir William Halcrow & Partners
Quantity Surveyor **Gleeds Quantity Surveyors**
Photography **Tom Miller (montage)**
Programme **1996–2000**

Future Systems

Media Centre, Lord's Cricket Ground, London

At Lord's, a tradition of patronage exists for innovative structures. The objective of the design of the new Media Centre is to respect the essential nature of Lord's while bringing to it a building that will herald the coming millennium and provide the most elegant and state-of-the-art media centre in the world. Just as sports equipment and the game of cricket have evolved, so too must the form of the buildings associated with it.

The new Media Centre will be the first all-aluminium, semi-monocoque building in the world. This extraordinary concept represents a breakthrough, not just in the creation of a new three-dimensional aesthetic, but in its method of construction: The building will be constructed by a boatyard, using the very latest advances in boat-building technology. The aerodynamic contours of the building reflect the sweep of the plan of the Ground with the enclosing skin formed by a smooth, gently-curved, white, seamless shell. The west-facing glazing is inclined to avoid any glare or reflections while providing unobstructed views of the game for up to 250 journalists and photographers.

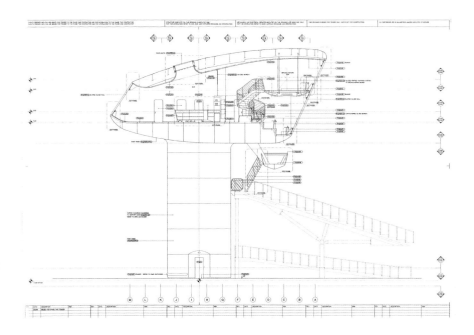

Client **Marylebone Cricket Club**

Architect **Future Systems**

Structural Engineer **Ove Arup & Partners**

Services Engineer **Buro Happold**

Quantity Surveyor **Davis Langdon & Everest**

Project Managers **Gardiner & Theobald Management Services**

Photography Images **Future Systems**

Programme **Completion: Summer 1998**

David Marks Julia Barfield Architects

British Airways Millennium Wheel, London

The British Airways Millennium Wheel is to be built
on the banks of the River Thames opposite the Houses
of Parliament. From the end of 1999, for a period of
five years, millions of visitors will be able to enjoy un-
paralleled views over one of the world's most celebrated
and historically rich cities.

Described as London's answer to Paris' Eiffel Tower,
the 500-foot diametre wheel will carry visitors in sixty
enclosed passenger capsules for a spectacular "flight
over the heart of the capital." The highest observation
wheel in the world, it will be a demonstration of the use
of renewable energy; solar cells will be built into the
passenger capsules and will help power the ventilation,
lighting and communication systems.

The design team investigated over 100 permutations of
cable configurations and rim depth. It was discovered
that more cables meant a narrower and smaller rim.
The structure of the wheel consists of a circular steel
truss connected to the hub by twenty pairs of pre-
stressed cables. A further sixteen cables, grouped in
fours, run from the hub to the rim's outer face. These
prevent the rim from twisting out of shape. The wheel
will be turned by its rim, using two motors sited at
either end of the boarding platform.

The wheel is a joint venture between British Airways
and the Millennium Wheel Company. No public funds
are being called for.

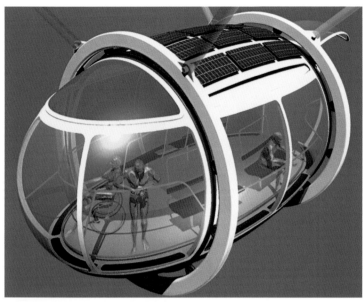

Client **British Airways and the Millennium Wheel Company**
Architects **David Marks Julia Barfield Architects**
Structural Engineer **Ove Arup & Partners**
Quantity Surveyor **Gardiner & Theobald**
Project Manager **PDCM**
M&E Services Engineer **Loren Butt**
Landscape Architect **Edward Hutchinson Landscape Architects**
CAD Image **Hayes Davidson**
Models **Andrew Ingham & Associates**
Photography **Nick Wood**
Programme **February 1998–September 1999**

Richard Rogers Partnership

Millennium Experience, Greenwich, London

After a national competition in February 1996 with fifty-seven competing locations, the Millennium Commission selected Greenwich to be the site for the National Millennium Experience. Occupied by a former gasworks, the 181-acre site had been derelict for more than two decades, and is the largest undeveloped area on the River Thames. The land was sold by British Gas to English Partnership, a government regeneration body who appointed the Richard Rogers Partnership to draw up a masterplan for the 300-acre peninsula which is to include the development of 5,000 houses, a business district and industrial retail areas.

The centrepiece of Lord Rogers' masterplan will be the Millennium Dome, designed in conjunction with the designers Imagination Ltd. and the structural engineers Buro Happold. The Dome will be 320 metres in diametre and, at its centre, fifty metres high. It will be suspended from a series of twelve, 100-metre steel masts, held in place by more than seventy kilometres of high-strength cable. The Dome will have a circumference of one kilometre and a ground floor of over 80,000 sq.m., making it the largest building of this type in the world.

The Millennium Experience will run for at least a year, possibly longer, depending on the success of the events. The building could last for decades; the glass-fibre roof has a life expectancy of at least twenty-five years and the steel masts could last up to sixty years. With maintenance and repairs the building could survive well into the next century. Several after-use proposals have been discussed for the Dome – including using it as a site for major sports development, an educational or entertainment centre or as a conference hall.

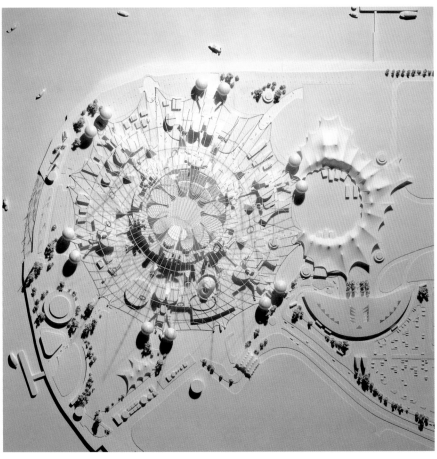

Client **English Partnerships**

Architect **Richard Rogers Partnership**

Exhibitions Designers **Imagination Ltd**

Structural Engineer **Buro Happold**

Consulting Engineers **Thorburn Colquhoun and Cundall Johnston & Partners**

M&E Services Engineer **Buro Happold**

Civil Engineer **WS Atkins**

Quantity Surveyor **McAlpine/Laing**

Contractor **McAlpine/Laing**

Environmental Consultant **Battle McCarthy**

CAD Image **Hayes Davidson**

Models **In-house Model Shop**

Photography **Eamonn O'Mahony, Richard Davies**

Cost **£40m for the dome structure**

Programme **1997–autumn 1998**

Alsop and Störmer Architects
Peckham Library and Media Centre, London

Armstrong Architects
La Maison de la Culture du Japon, Paris

Behnisch, Behnisch and Partner
Harbourside Centre for the Performing Arts,
Bristol

Benson and Forsyth
Museum of Scotland, Edinburgh

Architekturbüro Bolles-Wilson & Partner
Library, Münster

Branson Coates Architecture
National Centre for Popular Music, Sheffield

David Chipperfield Architects
Competition Proposal for the Centre for
Performing Arts, Bristol

David Chipperfield Architects
Neues Museum, Berlin

Foster and Partners
British Museum Redevelopment, London

Nicholas Grimshaw and Partners
National Space Science Centre, Leicester

Zaha M. Hadid
Luxembourg Concert Hall

Herzog & de Meuron
Tate Gallery of Modern Art, Bankside, London

Levitt Bernstein Associates
Corn Exchange, King's Lynn

Daniel Libeskind
Imperial War Museum – North, Manchester

Daniel Libeskind
V & A Museum Boilerhouse Extension, London

MacCormac Jamieson Prichard
The Wellcome Wing at the Science Museum,
London

Pringle Richards Sharratt Architects
V & A Millennium Gallery and Winter-Garden,
Sheffield

Ian Ritchie Architects
Tower Bridge Theatre, London

Richard Rogers Partnership
South Bank Centre Redevelopment, London

Michael Wilford and Partners
Lowry Centre, Salford

Colin St John Wilson and Partners
British Library, St Pancras, London

Culture

20th-century British architecture has yielded many significant public, transport and commercial buildings, yet there are few contemporary arts buildings of architectural distinction. The Royal Festival Hall (Leslie Martin, 1951) and the National Theatre (Denys Lasdun, 1970) in London are rare post-1945 exemplars, with smaller but significant interventions such as Norman Foster's Sackler Galleries at the Royal Academy and James Stirling's Clore Gallery extension at the Tate Gallery. But all this is set to change.

Since 1994, a vast investment in the cultural fabric of the nation has been made possible by the introduction of the National Lottery. This bi-weekly number game attracts millions of citizens to gamble in the hope of winning a substantial cash prize. Half the proceeds of the Lottery are given out in prizes, but the other half is being funnelled into new arts, cultural and sports buildings, as well as the refurbishment of the nation's architectural heritage. Over £2 billion has been invested in opera houses, football and rugby stadia, cultural centres and art galleries, museums, monuments and cathedrals. Most of these projects are the subject of design competitions, giving quality of design a priority for this new generation of buildings funded by 'the people's money'.

This investment has coincided with a particularly vibrant period of British artistic production in the 1990s. Visual art, contemporary dance, music and architecture are at a peak, receiving international critical and popular acclaim. Many of the new buildings featured in this exhibition will house these cultural activities, providing a British response to the high levels of public investment in the arts witnessed over the last decade in other European countries. In France, Spain and Germany – in particular – there has been a sustained investment in culture. The French "Grands Projets" – including the "Très Grande Bibilothèque", the Cité de la Musique and the Maison du Japon in Paris – are matched in terms of public patronage by the new generation of museums realised in Frankfurt,

Stuttgart and other German cities in the 1980s. Equally inspired examples can be found throughout Spain and Scandinavia. In all these cases, cultural buildings have played a significant role in the economy and identity of individual city states.

The idiosyncratic nature of arts programmes has given rise to a highly diverse range of new designs that will, over the next ten years, transform Britain's cultural map. New or refurbished museums and galleries in London, Glasgow, Manchester and Sheffield – by some of the country's most talented architects – will attract new audiences, satisfying the growing appetite for culture and information. These buildings are representative of a Europe-wide trend, where investment in cultural buildings is considered to have clear social and economic benefits, stimulating local creative industries and contributing to the quality of life of the inner city.

London's new Tate Gallery of Modern Art in a disused power station at Bankside, designed by the Swiss architects Herzog & de Meuron, will be a pristine and rigorous adaptation of an existing structure that will contribute significantly to the regeneration of a run-down inner city area. Over two million people will visit the building when it opens in the year 2000, one of the first *grands projets* to celebrate the millennium. In Bristol, the German architects Behnisch, Behnisch and Partner are building a highly expressive Performing Arts Centre along the city's industrial waterfront, while in the heart of Victorian London, the Polish-American deconstructivist Daniel Libeskind is planning an articulated and multifaceted extension to the sombre Victoria & Albert Museum. The National Lottery has fortunately opened the doors to non-British architects and designers, who are contributing a richer architectural vocabulary to the British urban landscape.

Alsop and Störmer Architects

Peckham Library and Media Centre, London

Together with the existing Peckham Arch and Health & Fitness Centre, the new Peckham Library and Media Centre will form the setting for the new Peckham Square, part of a larger scheme for the regeneration of Peckham.

The main lending library consists of a large double-height space raised twelve metres above ground level, supported on one side by angled steel columns, on the other by a vertical block in which a bookshop, vertical circulation, staff facilities and a multi-media training centre. Floating within the double-height of the lending library are three 'pods' which provide accommodation for the children's activities area, the Afro-Caribbean literature centre and a meeting room.

At ground level, a new covered public space is being created which will be used to stage open-air events. The elevations are clad in patinated green copper, coloured and clear structural glass and expanded mesh panels.

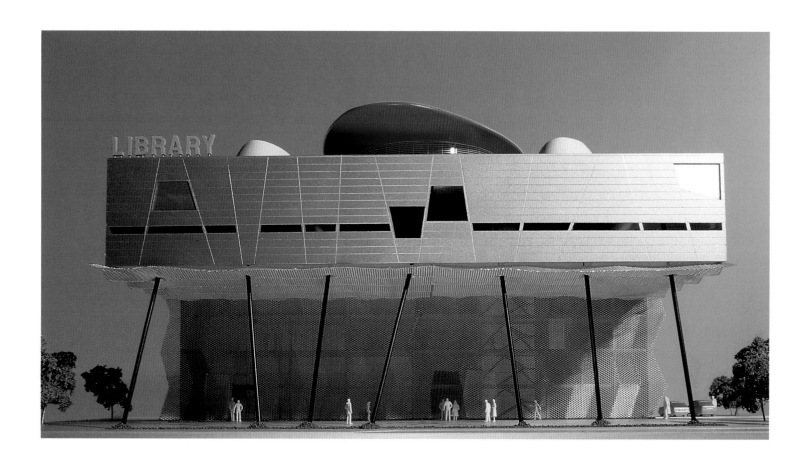

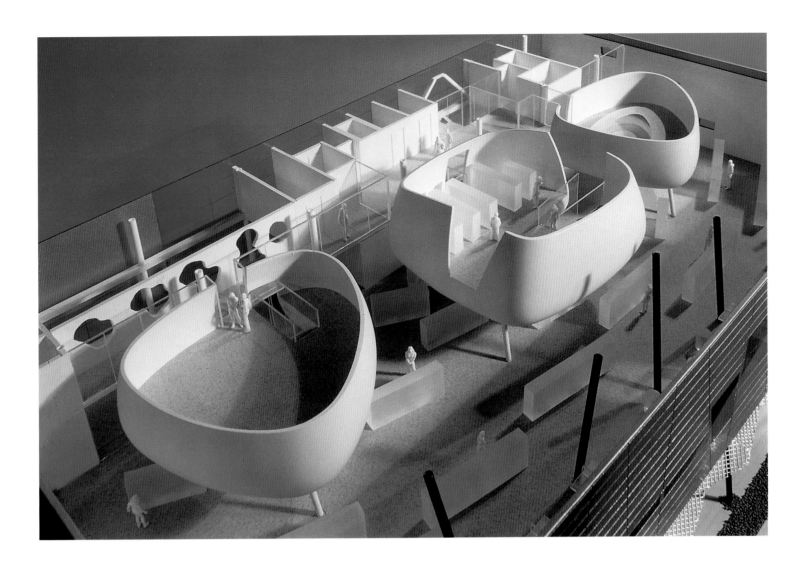

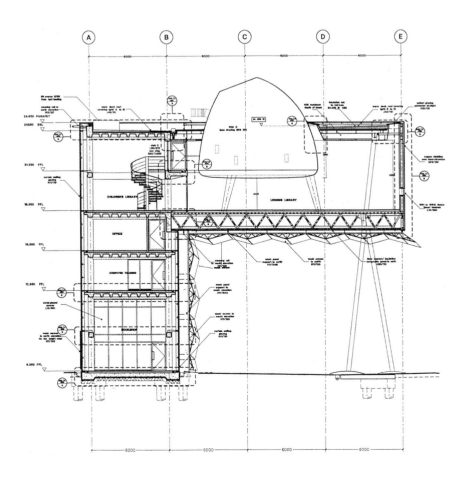

Client **Southwark Education and Leisure Department**

Architects **Alsop & Störmer Architects**

Project Manager **Southwark Building Design Services**

Structural Engineers **Adams Kara Taylor Engineers**

Environmental Engineers **Battle McCarthy Engineers**

Quantity Surveyor **Franklin & Andrews**

Acoustic Engineers, **Applied Acoustic Design**

Photography **Roderick Coyne**

Cost **£4.2m**

Programme **1997–99**

Armstrong Architects

La Maison de la Culture du Japon, Paris

This project brings to Paris its first purpose-built Japanese cultural institute. Accommodation includes a restaurant, tea-house, mediathèque, library, exhibition hall, shop, seminar rooms and theatre.

The building can be perceived above ground level as the bow of a sail, with its main glass facade tightly trimmed to the curved street boundary. Where it curves to a point, it becomes a suspended glass screen, inviting the public to enter the building via a small courtyard. The internal arrangement of 'servant' flanking 'served' spaces and clearly defined circulation routes emphasises the hierarchy of public and private, relating interior experiences to framed exterior views to the Eiffel Tower and across the River Seine.

The geometry of the upper levels is continued below ground to the transformable multipurpose hall which can provide numerous theatre configurations including 'Kabuki', and 'Noh', as well as those of the proscenium arch, concert hall, cinema and ballroom.

The design attempts to resolve and integrate the multiple functions of the building on a restricted urban site into a harmonious and ordered whole, using simple geometrical forms and a restricted palette of materials to form a restrained backdrop to the multitude of activities contained within.

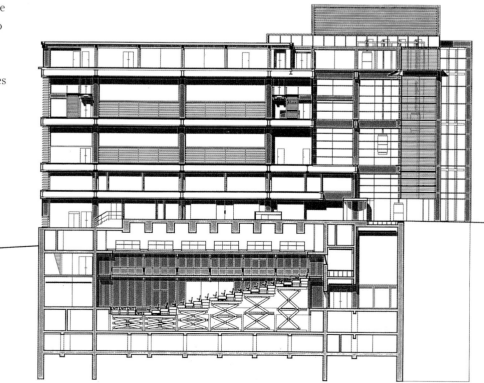

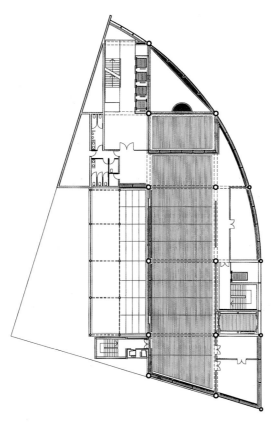

Client **The Japan Foundation**

Architect **Armstrong Architects**

Structural Engineer **Groupe Arcora**

Services Engineer **Trouvin Ingenerie**

Cost Consultant **Algoe**

Project Managers **Shimizu France; Scic Amo**

Theatre Consultant **Scene**

Theatre Contractor **AMG**

Fire Consultant **Casso**

Acoustic Consultant **Xu Acoustics**

Main Contractor **Quillery**

Photography **Didier Boy de la Tour**

Cost **FF 180m**

Programme **1991 (competition)–1997**

Behnisch, Behnisch and Partner

Harbourside Centre for the Performing Arts, Bristol

This building will contribute a special, sculptural shape which not only focuses attention on the Harbourside Centre itself but also, by contrast, heightens the qualities of other harbourside buildings. The complexity of the exterior alters the scale of the building depending on whether viewed from the harbour, from street level or from the higher ground on the outskirts of the city.

The volume is divided into three principal elements: an administration/educational facilities building, a concert hall and a dance theatre. These elements are not individually evident from the exterior because they are united under one large, common roof and below by an open concourse level. However, because of their discreet arrangement, operational, technical and acoustical separation is possible. The physical separation also lends the building a significant transparency at the main entrance. From this entrance foyer, visitors can indirectly experience the atmosphere of the harbour from a new city square.

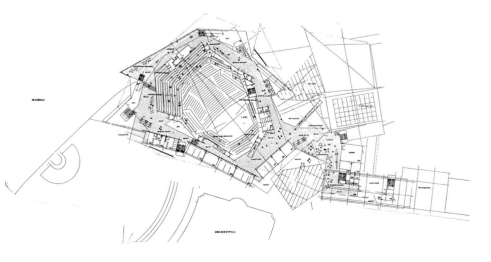

Client **Bristol Harbourside Centre**

Architect **Behnisch, Behnisch & Partner**

Structural and Civil Engineers **Buro Happold with Schlaich, Bergermann & Partner**

M&E Services Engineer **Max Fordham & Partners**

Cost Consultant **Gleeds**

Theatre Consultants **Theatre Projects Consultants**

Lighting Consultant **Barton Bach Licht Labor**

Acoustics **BBM Müller**

Fire Engineering **Buro Happold**

Models **Behnisch, Behnisch & Partner**

Photography **Behnisch, Behnisch & Partner**

Cost **£55m**

Programme **1997–2002**

Benson and Forsyth

Museum of Scotland, Edinburgh

The brief was for a building to be fully integrated with and entered through the existing Royal Museum of Scotland, therefore reconciling the change of scale and expression between the horizontally-organised museum and the diminutive vertical houses clustered around. This is achieved by wrapping a lower outer building, which contains the study galleries and temporary exhibition, around the higher rectilinear main gallery and the triangular entrance space. The corner of Chambers Street is redefined by a cylindrical form which addresses the five approach streets, while providing an independent entrance and a non-specific gallery space.

Internally, the entrance to the new museum is on the main axis of the magnificent original luminous hall. A second connection is made by extending the line of the colonnade into the base of the triangulated hall, conceived as a terminal space. A large opening in the outer wall at the focus of the space addresses the entrance to Greyfriars opposite.

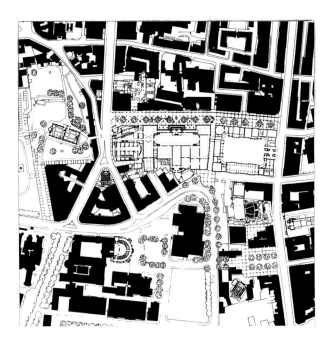

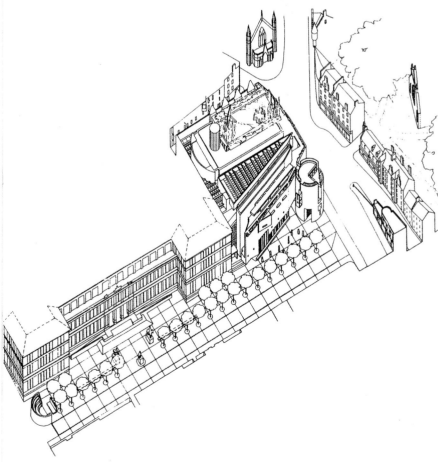

Client **The Board of Trustees of the National Museums of Scotland**

Architect **Benson and Forsyth**

Structural Engineer **Anthony Hunt Associates**

Services Engineer **Waterman Gore**

Quantity Surveyor **Davis Langdon & Everest**

Lighting Consultant **Kevan Shaw Lighting**

Building Control Consultant **Butler & Young Associates**

Cost **£34m**

Programme **To be completed November 1998**

Architekturbüro Bolles-Wilson & Partner

Library, Münster

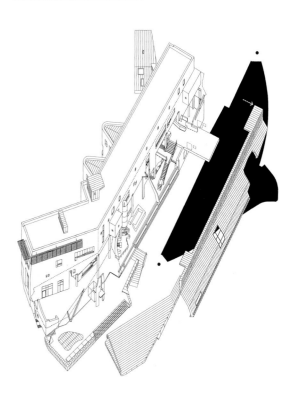

This new library takes its place confidently between the original library (Krameramtshaus 1589) and Kiffe Pavilion (1950s). The building is cut in two by a new pedestrian street, the open facades being re-enclosed by two large, sloping copper walls; below these are concentrated internal lines of movement on both sides of the passage. Light from above reflects from the wooden-panelled internal face of these walls. Glass strips below expose the entire ground level to the passer-by who, even before entering, is standing at the centre of the new library.

The library is the first in Germany to tackle the question of the changing status of information. The result is the Three Zone Library: the Far Zone is long-term storage (no public access); the Middle Zone is the lending library, the realm of the book. What is new here is the Near Zone, the library as an information supermarket. This zone is connected to the Middle Zone only via the first floor bridge, on which is situated the main information desk, and in the basement (Sound Library) where the two buildings become one. Café, exhibition and newspaper-reading salon are in the unsupervised area at the entrance; two floors of offices are situated above.

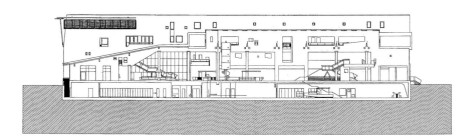

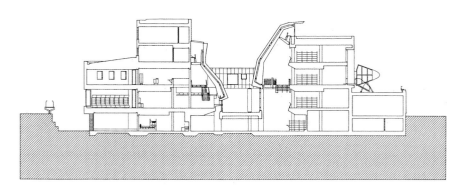

Client **Stadt Münster**
Architect **Architekturbüro Bolles-Wilson & Partner**
Structural Engineer **Ing. Büro Thomas Münster**
M&E Services Engineer **Ing. Büro Albers, Münster and**
Hochbauamt Münster
Surveyor **Assmann Planning, Münster**
Lighting **Licht Design, Cologne**
Models **Bolles-Wilson**
Photography **Christian Richters**
Cost **DM 47.5m**

Branson Coates Architecture

National Centre for Popular Music, Sheffield

Branson Coates liken their design for the new National Centre for Popular Music to a jukebox, allowing for randomly accessible events. Situated in Sheffield's rapidly expanding cultural industries quarter, the scheme consists of four drums which will house the four main elements of the exhibition programme in their upper storeys. These comprise an interactive exhibition gallery celebrating the history and development of popular music; a practical display area exploring the mechanics of how popular music is created, recorded and distributed; a sound arena where art and technology combine to create musical environments; and a gallery for temporary exhibitions.

The glazed interstitial crossing between the four drums acts as the inter-connecting public foyer and coincides with the paths of the city. Visually, the drums are abstractly reminiscent of great industrial structures that were familiar in the Sheffield landscape. Each drum is clad in stainless steel and the undercut at street level glazed to intensify the urban relationship of the cafés and shops. The four top cowls rotate slowly in the wind to provide natural low energy ventilation.

The National Centre for Popular Music is supported by the National Lottery through the Arts Council of England, and is in part financed by English Partnership and the European Community's European Regional Development Fund.

Client **Music Heritage Limited**
Architect **Branson Coates Architecture**
Project Management **Bucknall Austin Project Management**
Structural Engineer **Buro Happold**
Environmental Services Engineer **Max Fordham & Partners**
Quantity Surveyor **Davis Langdon & Everest**
Contractor **Higgs and Hill Northern Ltd**
Photography **Andrew Putler**
Cost **The overall project cost is £ 15m;
the building cost is £ 8.5m**
Programme **1996–98**

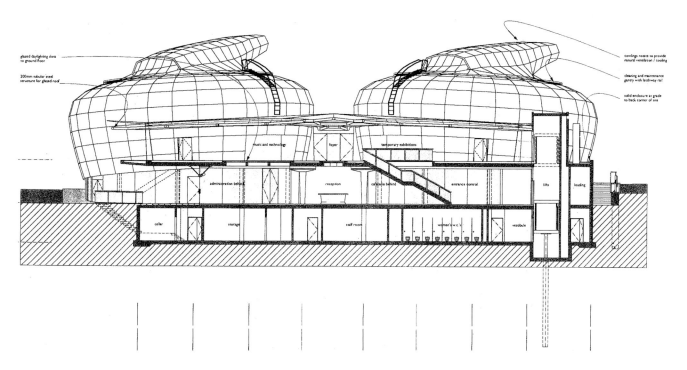

David Chipperfield Architects

Competition Proposal for the Centre for Performing Arts, Bristol

The proposed building needed to be of great scale, but its materiality, texture and openness were to maintain the spirit of the harbourside location. Scale and material were interwoven by interlocking wooden boxes that not only celebrate the heroic scale of the building form, but, by its assemblage of smaller elements of great materiality, restore it to human proportions.

The building established two physical propositions; an external wooden frame, acting as a tectonic structure, and an internal plastic mass, responding to the organic development of the auditorium. The interstitial space, between the external wooden boxes and the internal mass, houses public circulation and hospitality functions.

Detached from the external skin, the auditorium shell and associated formal and organisational circulation is free to float within the fragile wooden boxes. The two layers of the facade and the play of light confront the problem of the blank auditoria. The interplay between the two volumes, the changing effect of light and the paradox of a transparent mass ensures a building of poetic possibility. The minimal architecture of Chipperfield's proposal is in stark contrast to the winning scheme by Behnisch, Behnisch and Partner (see pages 112–113).

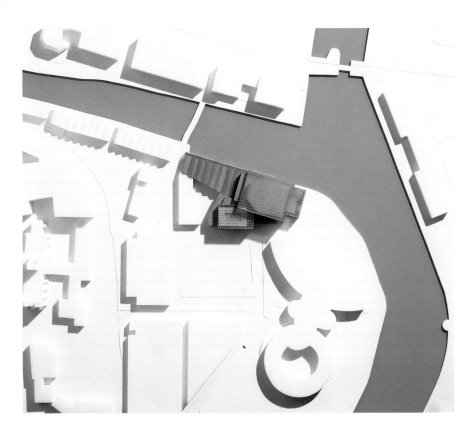

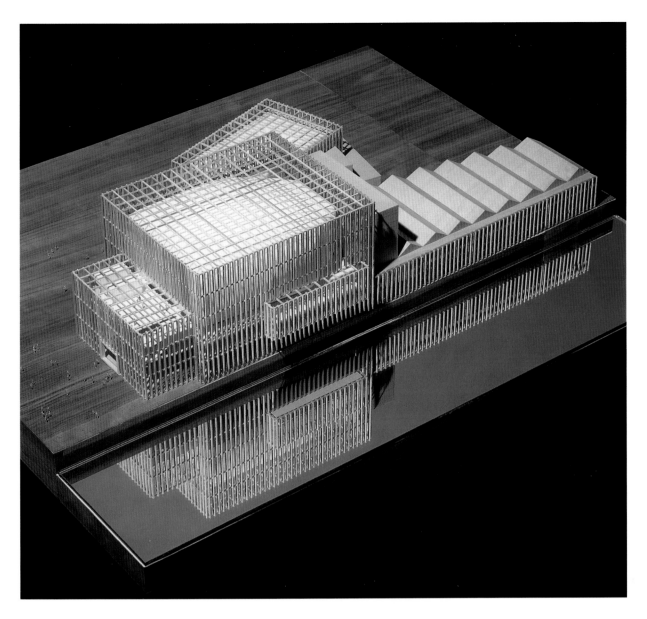

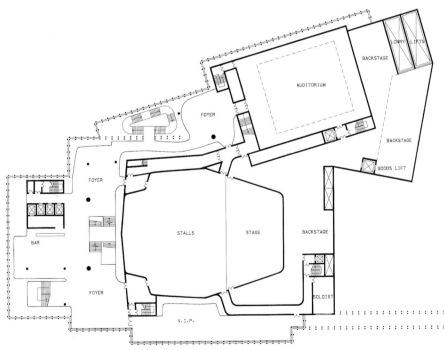

Architect **David Chipperfield Architects**

Structural, Services and Acoustic Engineers
Ove Arup & Partners

Quantity Surveyor **Tim Gatehouse Associates**

Photographer **Richard Davies**

Programme **1996 (design)**

David Chipperfield Architects

Neues Museum, Berlin

As a literal reconstruction of the Neues Museum would be unacceptable, the intention is to add to it, giving a clear significance to the building – the culmination of Greek Revival Architecture in the late nineteenth century, standing alongside Schinkel's Altes Museum. It was clear that the building must be a collage of its own initial splendour, its historical damage and powerful interventions signalling a new future for the structure. This 'collage' approach allows the co-existence of layers and is fundamental to the future significance of the monument. Rather than impose a formal structure on the project, a series of separate investigations around the main issues have been pursued. This approach allows the contradictory concerns expressed by the organisational brief and those maintained by the conservationists to be taken into consideration. Conclusions were presented as works in progress, establishing principles rather than solutions.

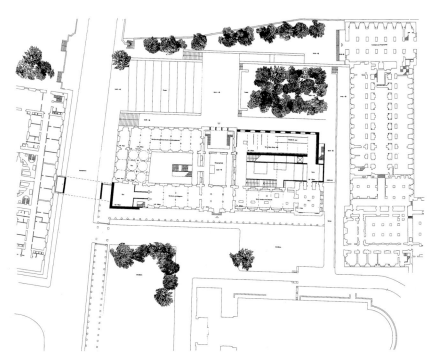

Client **Bundesbaudirektion, Berlin**

Architect **David Chipperfield Architects**

Historical Consultant **Julian Harrap Architects**

Structural Engineer **Ove Arup & Partners; Jane Wernick**

Service Engineers **Ove Arup & Partners (London; Berlin)**

Photography **Stefan Müller (existing building);**

Richard Davies (model)

Cost **£100m**

Programme **1997–2003**

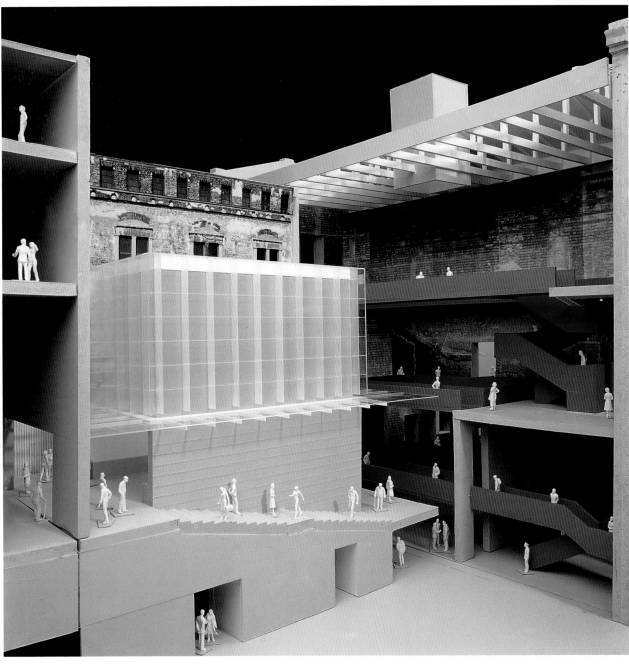

Foster and Partners

British Museum Redevelopment, London

The departure of the British Library from the central inner courtyard and the domed Reading Room of the British Museum provides an opportunity to recapture this lost space. The Great Court will be enclosed with a lightweight glazed roof and entered from the principal level of the Museum. The Museum's Centre for Education and new ethnographic galleries will be located beneath this main level. Bookshops, restaurants and cafés will be on Level 2 and mezzanine levels above. These mezzanines, elliptical in plan, are centred on the Reading Room. A pair of great staircases, which form a processional route linking the Court to the upper galleries of the Museum, encircle the restored drum of the Reading Room.

The original facades of the courtyard will also be restored and the southern portico reinstated. The new space, with its light-transmitting roof, will complement the 19th-century architecture of the Museum.

Client **British Museum Development Trust**
Architect **Foster and Partners**
Structural Engineer **Buro Happold**
Quantity Surveyor **Davis Langdon & Everest**
Photography **Richard Davies**
Programme **1997–2000**

Nicholas Grimshaw and Partners

National Space Science Centre, Leicester

The main exhibition space is created by floating a new roof plane over the existing underground storm water tanks on the site, which are to be retained and converted. The roof is raised above ground level to allow light into the perimeter accommodation, while slots within it define the circulation routes and light the exhibits below. The roof is designed as a tanked, shallow pool, reflecting the forms of the building by day and illuminated at night. The domes that penetrate the surface of the roof plane mirror the forms of the planetarium and observatory below.

The geometrical orientation of the landscaping is generated by the gently-descending ramped entrance to the centre, highlighted by the creation of a new exhibition tower. The tower is designed both as a fitting climax to the exhibition itself and as a demonstration of different technologies and their potential role in future space developments. A combination of materials is used to create the skin enclosure, while the shield element to the south and west provides an intelligent glass facade. The components of the glass wall are electrically-active, powered by photo-voltaic cells on the shield. These turn the glass opaque and reflect the sun's heat during summer, while in winter the glass remains clear and allows views out.

Client **Leicester City Council and University of Leicester**
Architect **Nicholas Grimshaw and Partners**
Structural Engineer **Ove Arup & Partners**
M&E Services Engineer **Ove Arup & Partners**
Quantity Surveyor **Beard Dove**
Landscape Architect **Land Use Consultants**
Models **Network Modelmakers**
Photography **Michael Dyer Associates**
Cost **£45m**
Programme **1997–99**

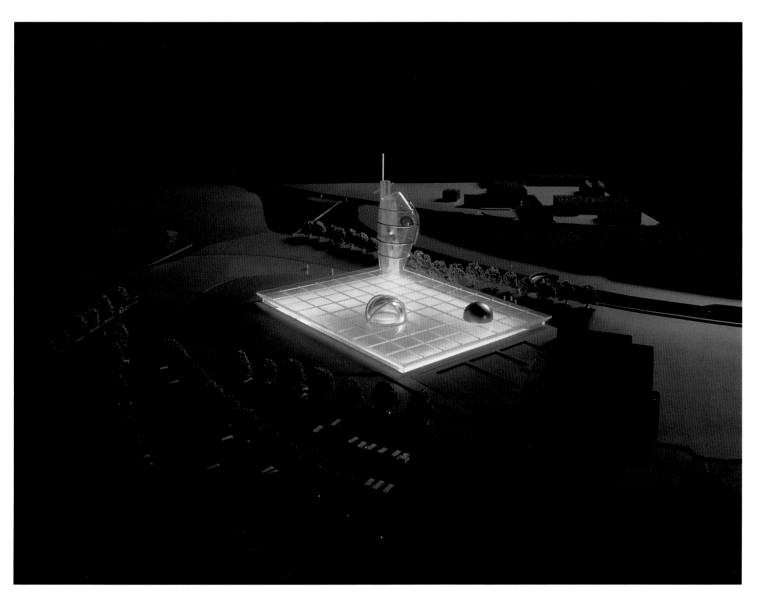

Zaha M. Hadid

Luxembourg Concert Hall

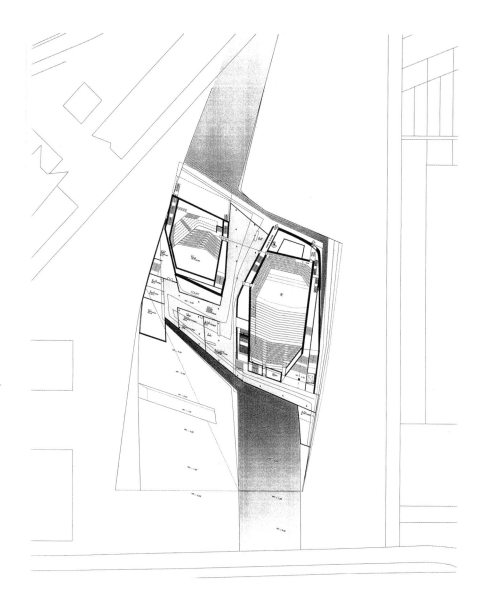

The design develops its tectonic language as an interpretation and extension of the animated topography of the Kirchberg. Slopes, cliffs and valleys articulate a programme with diverse sectional requirements. The two main event spaces – the concert hall and the chamber music hall – stand out in sharp relief as the main 'scenic' features. The rehearsal spaces announce themselves indirectly: a large plate lifts up to give space underneath. The whole coheres into an artificial mountain crowning the plateau of the Place d'Europe. The public arriving at the plateau ascends further to the raised foyer level of the concert hall. Upon entry, the halls themselves are then experienced as valleys into which one descends.

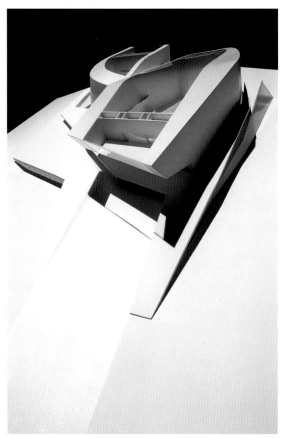

Client **Ministry of Public Buildings, Luxembourg**
Architect **Zaha M. Hadid**
Project Architect **Patrik Schumacher**
Structural Engineer **Ove Arup & Partners**
Acoustic Engineer **Arup Acoustics**
Theatre Consultant **Anne Minors**
Quantity Surveyor **Davis Langdon & Everest**
Photography **Edward Woodman**
Cost **£ 27m**
Programme **1997 (design)**

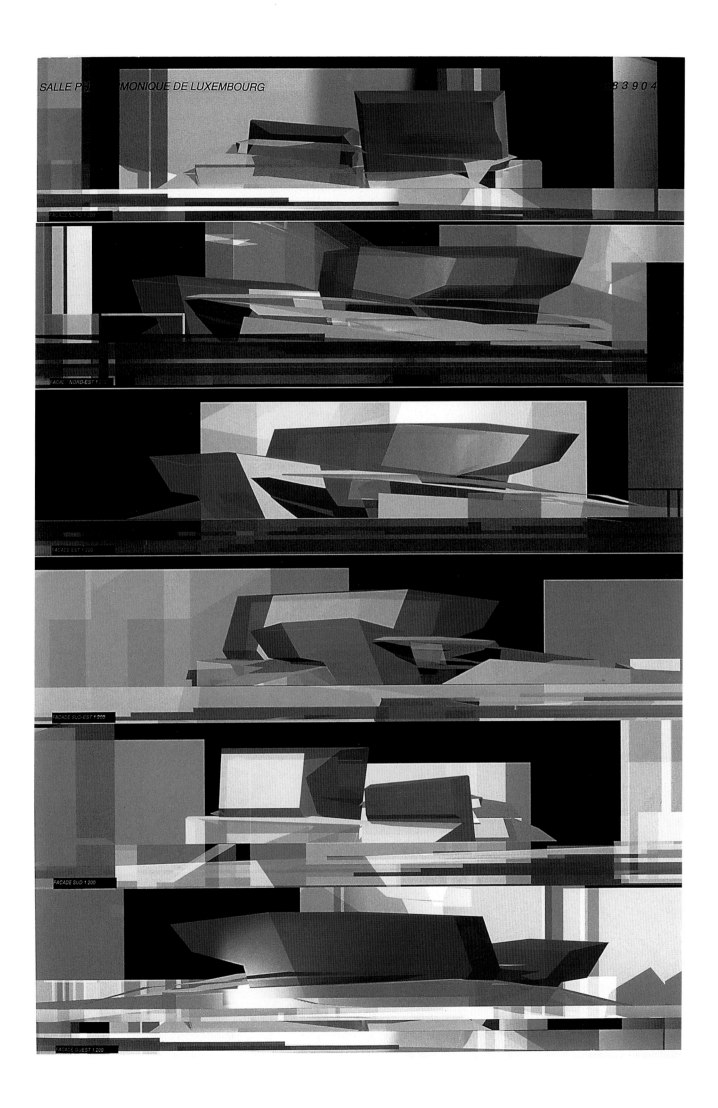

SALLE PHILHARMONIQUE DE LUXEMBOURG

FACADE NORD 1:200

FACADE NORD-EST 1:200

FACADE EST 1:200

FACADE SUD-EST 1:200

FACADE SUD 1:200

FACADE OUEST 1:200

129

Herzog & de Meuron

Tate Gallery of Modern Art, Bankside, London

The existing power station, designed by the architect Sir Giles Scott, is a historic landmark on the River Thames. The Swiss architects Herzog & de Meuron's proposal for its conversion into the Tate Gallery of Modern Art will retain the building's existing architectural qualities, while at the same time adding something powerful and contemporary. The Turbine Hall will be turned into one of London's most impressive covered public spaces, comparable to a *galleria* with a unique industrial appearance. The outside of the brick building will express the different activities offered in the new museum which are all about looking, perception and communication. The most noticeable change to the exterior is the glass structure spanning the length of the roof, which adds two floors and allows natural light into the galleries below.

The new gallery will be a place of encounter of man and works of art – a very simple idea which has often been neglected in the architectural concept of recent museums. Six suites of rooms on three levels will offer a wide variety of spatial experience: rooms of different sizes with different wall heights, punctuated by glass windows giving views both into and out of the galleries. 'Found' exhibition spaces, such as the former oil tanks, will add to this variety. The main entrance into the building is a ramp into the former Turbine Hall. There is an additional entrance on either side of the chimney on the north side.

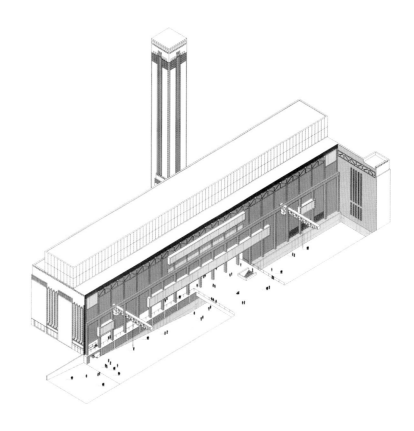

Client **The Tate Gallery**

Architect **Herzog & de Meuron**

Associate Architect **Sheppard Robson**

Structural M&E Services Engineer **Ove Arup & Partners**

Quantity Surveyor **Davis Langdon & Everest**

CAD Image **Hayes Davidson**

Cost **£130m**

Programme **Completion: Spring 2000**

Levitt Bernstein Associates

Corn Exchange, King's Lynn

This Grade 2 listed building dates from 1854 and was in a dilapidated state. After a limited competition, Levitt Bernstein Associates were appointed to create a performance space as phase one of the scheme. It is intended to further develop the site into an arts centre, which will include two theatres fronting the river. King's Lynn Corn Exchange has been transformed from a flat floor hall into a multi-purpose space seating 744, suitable for concerts as well as for other community events. A new 'over roof' structure rests on external columns and covers two-thirds of the original hall above the new auditorium and stage, solving structural, servicing and acoustic problems. The original glazed roof has been restored above the foyer and simulated within the auditorium by an acoustically transparent mesh ceiling. The design makes a clear distinction between existing building features and new interventions. Three commissioned artworks have been incorporated into the building programme.

Client **Borough Council of King's Lynn & West Norfolk**
Architect **Levitt Bernstein Associates**
Structural Engineer **Michael Barclay Partnership**
M&E Services Engineer and Acoustician **Max Fordham & Partners**
Quantity Surveyor **Bucknall Austin**
Theatre Consultant **Carr and Angier**
Lighting Consultant **Equation Lighting Design**
Contractor **Sindall Norwich Ltd.**
Disability Access **All Clear Designs**
Photography **Matthew Weinreb**
Cost **£3.5m**
Programme **Design from April 1994, on site from May 1995,
performances started September 1997**

Daniel Libeskind

The Imperial War Museum – North, Manchester

The internal space of the proposed Imperial War Museum is an open volume in the form of the Earth's curvature, giving immediate orientation in the museum as well as relating the project to other events across the world. The relationship between the uninterrupted flow of the museum and the external landscape is mediated by the structure of the 'world' itself in its 24-hour time sequence. The time and space dimension of the museum allows for easy orientation as to the place of conflict, and shows the tension between visible conflict and its historical infrastructure.

The sail-like shelves with their outdoor exhibitions are dramatically related to the surrounding landscape, the Ship Canal, the Lowry Centre (see pages 146–147) and Manchester United's football ground. The simplicity of the actual museum space and its extensive expression is conceived as an economical and basic concrete-and-steel structure with a maximum flow of light and air and a minimisation of maintenance cost.

While it is easy to get lost in the details of organising the vast quantitative history of the 20th century, the museum will still project itself into the consciousness of the visitor as an unforgettable synthetic experience, integrating the flowering of culture in permanent relationship with the shattering groundlessness which war and violence bring to the world.

Client **The Imperial War Museum**
Architect **Daniel Libeskind Architectural Studio**
Design and Engineering Consultant **Ove Arup & Partners**
Quantity Surveyor **Davis, Langdon & Everest**
Landscape Consultant **Müller, Knippschild, Wehberg**
Exhibition Design **Stephen Greenberg, DEGW, Bob Baxter, Amalgam**
Photography **Bitter Bredt Fotografie**
Cost **£13.5m**
Programme **Completion 2001**

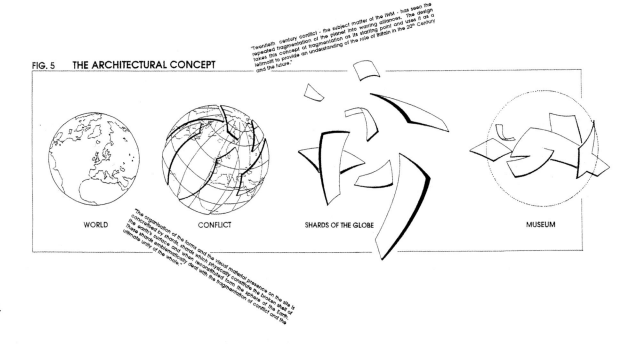

Twentieth century conflict - the subject matter of the IWM - has seen the repeated fragmentation of the planet into warring alliances. The design takes this concept of fragmentation as its starting point and uses it as a leitmotif to provide an understanding of the role of Britain in the 20th Century and the future.

FIG. 5   **THE ARCHITECTURAL CONCEPT**

The organisation of the forms and the visual material presence on the site is concretised by shards, shards which physically constitute the broken shell of the earth's surface and when reconstituted form the sphere of the Earth. These shards emblematically deal with the fragmentation of conflict and the ultimate unity of the whole.

WORLD   CONFLICT   SHARDS OF THE GLOBE   MUSEUM

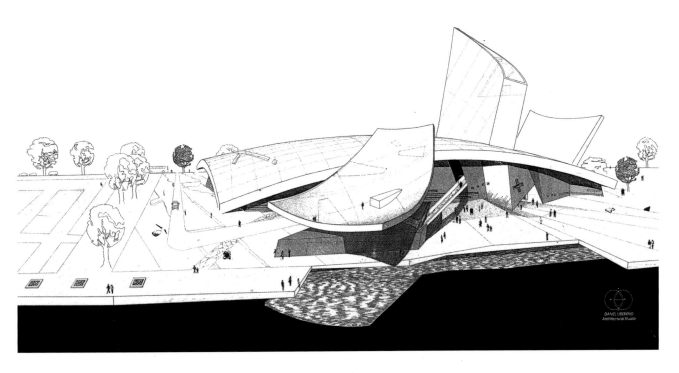

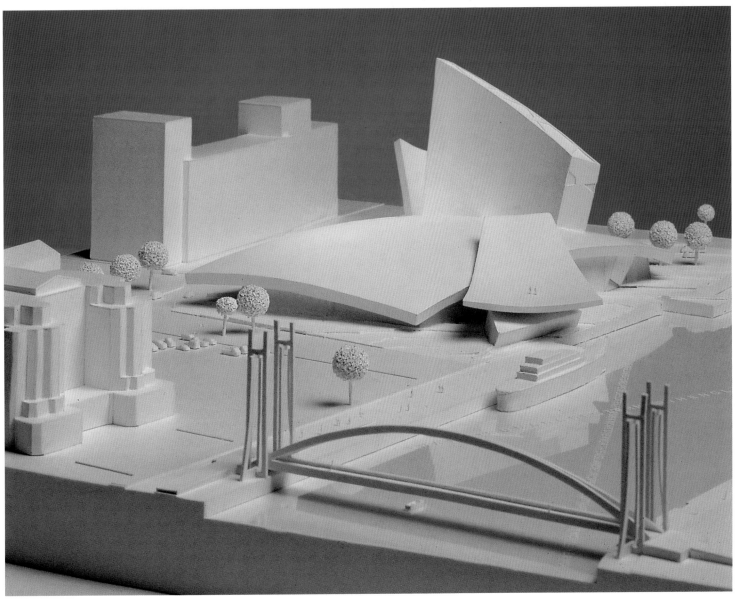

Daniel Libeskind

V & A Museum Boilerhouse Extension, London

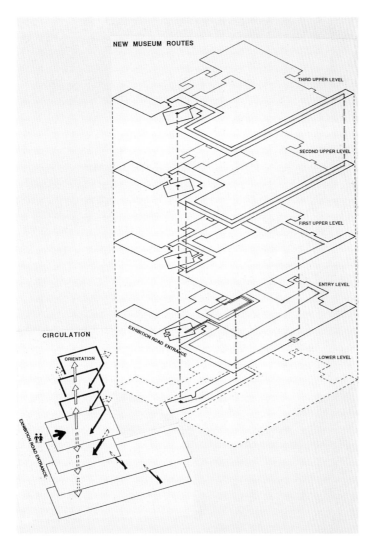

NEW MUSEUM ROUTES

THIRD UPPER LEVEL

SECOND UPPER LEVEL

FIRST UPPER LEVEL

ENTRY LEVEL

EXHIBITION ROAD ENTRANCE

LOWER LEVEL

CIRCULATION

ORIENTATION

EXHIBITION ROAD ENTRANCE

The design is structured around three dimensions: the spiral movement of art and history, the interlocking of inside and outside and the labyrinth of discovery. The first of these manifests itself in the overall form of the extension building and its circulation system, which implicates visitors in a spiral movement as they progress to the rest of the Museum, a counterpoint to the lateral, horizontal movement in the existing buildings.

The winding spiral creates an interlocking of inside and outside, bringing the visitor into close relation with history and the present, the city and the museum, through a direct experience of interpenetrating views and histories.

The labyrinth of discovery is the organizational leitmotif mediating between the existing galleries and the Museum's new programme requirements. The image of the labyrinth is not only a symbolic device, but a reinforcement of the unique qualities of the V & A; the cross-cultural collections, the multi-cultural profile of its visitors and the fusion of the arts, technology and history.

Client **The Victoria & Albert Museum**
Architect **Daniel Libeskind Architectural Studio**
Engineering and Design Consultants **Ove Arup & Partners**
Quantity Surveyor **Gardiner & Theobald**
Photography **Chris Duisberg, Manuel Herz, Marq Bailey**

MacCormac Jamieson Prichard

The Wellcome Wing at the Science Museum, London

The creation of the Wellcome Wing at the Science Museum presented a challenge; how to make a museum environment inherently flexible and adaptable, operationally efficient and easy to maintain. There are five principal components in the brief for the public areas of the new building, within a total area of 10,000 sq.m: exhibition space, central circulation, an IMAX cinema, catering and retail. A separate conference centre is to be built at the west end of the site.

The building is arranged as a single column-free volume, within which the exhibition floors and IMAX cinema are dramatically suspended, flanked by aisles which contain circulation, escape routes and servicing. The boundaries of the central volume are suffused with a deep blue light,

in which the IMAX and exhibition floors appear to float. The structure consists of concrete columns with steel trusses supported by gerberettes. The cantilevered gerberettes shorten the span of the trusses and substantially reduce their depth. Vertical tie rods in the external envelope restrain the cantilevers and transfer their load onto the foundations.

The design strategy maximises the future potential of the site by keeping the Wellcome Wing compact and placing the conference centre as a separate building on the frontage facing Queen's Gate.

The Wellcome Wing has been made possible by funding from The Wellcome Trust and the Heritage Lottery Fund.

Client **The Science Museum**
Architect **MacCormac Jamieson Prichard**
Contractor **Kier Build Ltd.**
Engineers **Ove Arup & Partners**
Quantity Surveyor **Davis Langdon & Everest**
Lighting Designer **Hollands Licht/Rogier van der Heide**
Photography **Steven Bedford – Virtual Artwork**

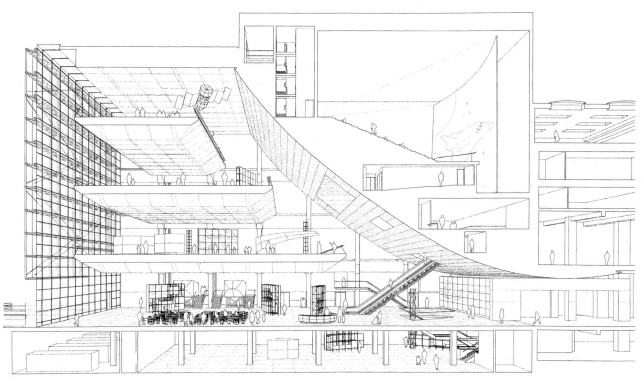

Drawing 1. Sectional perspective through exhibition area.

Pringle Richards Sharratt Architects

V & A Millennium Gallery and Winter-Garden, Sheffield

The gallery will be run in association with the Victoria & Albert Museum showing semi-permanent as well as temporary exhibitions, and is due to open in the year 2000 as part of the city's millennium celebrations.

Attached to the gallery will be a glazed winter-garden – a spectacular space, 24m wide and 24m high – which will provide an important amenity for the public in the city centre. It will be landscaped with winding paths, park benches, kiosks and hotel pavement cafés around the edge and a central space for open-air entertainment.

The buildings will be energy-efficient, utilising the winter-garden as a 'lung' through which surrounding buildings will breathe, tempering the air supply by pre-heating it in winter and using evaporative cooling from plants in summer. The gallery spaces will be roof-lit through a series of light reflectors within the structure zone.

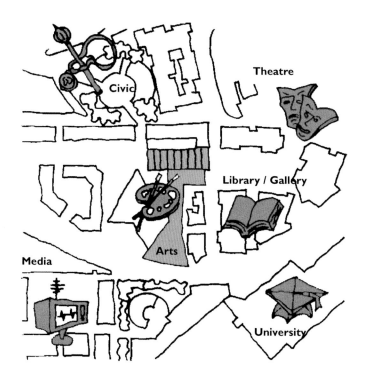

Client **City of Sheffield**

Architect **Pringle Richards Sharratt Architects**

Structural and Services Engineer **Buro Happold**

Quantity Surveyor **Design & Building Services,
Sheffield City Council**

Models **Network Modelmakers**

Photography **Richard Davies**

Cost **£13.7m**

Programme **1996–2000**

Ian Ritchie Architects

Tower Bridge Theatre, London

This theatre has been designed to accommodate the Royal Opera during the closure of the Royal Opera House for the redevelopment of its Covent Garden site. The theatre accommodates 2,350 people for opera, ballet and lyric productions, including rehearsal rooms, full back-up facilities and public café/library. The siting, form and external architecture have been influenced by this world heritage site adjacent to Tower Bridge and opposite the Tower of London.

The front of the building, facing across the Thames, is a colourless, vertical, double-glazed facade containing foyers at different levels, and an open-air terrace under the roof. The crystalline quality of the low-iron glass seeks to create a 'jewel case' facing the Tower.

The main body of the building appears solid, composed of woven stainless steel retaining stones, a finer grain at the base of the walls, and restrained by cables in a 'quilted' manner, punctuated by window openings formed by steel-plate assemblies. The use of woven stainless steel draws its inspiration from the Tower of London – a metaphor for medieval chain mail. The stone fill reflects the colour palette of the adjacent landmark structures – the restraining cables make reference to the suspension rods of Tower Bridge.

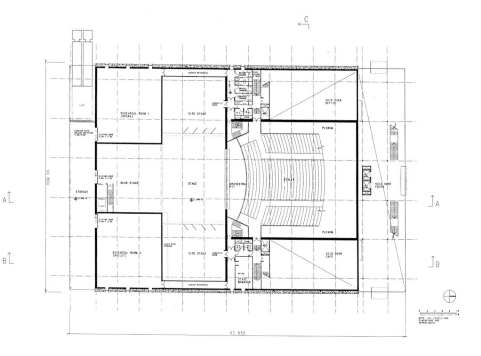

Client **Royal Opera House and Greater London Enterprise**
Architects and Interior Designers **Ian Ritchie Architects**
Structural and Services Engineers **Ove Arup & Partners**
Quantity Surveyor **Gardiner & Theobald**
Acoustic Engineers **Arup Acoustics**

Lighting **Ian Ritchie Architects**
Landscape **Ian Ritchie Architects**
Theatre Consultant **John Harrison, Technical Director, ROH**
Photography **Gaia**
Cost **£15.25m**

Richard Rogers Partnership

South Bank Centre Redevelopment, London

The South Bank Cultural Development is one of Europe's largest cultural clusters. It is beautifully positioned on the Thames, accessible from the North Bank, but very isolated by the big river itself. The Royal Festival Hall is one of the first major post-war buildings in Britain, and was later joined by a concert hall, a theatre and an exhibition gallery. However, the architecture was very much about objects rather than spaces, so the spaces are the "leftovers" with very strongly defined limits.

This design for revitalising the South Bank arts complex proposes an elegant, translucent canopy over the buildings to turn uninviting spaces into half-indoor/half-outdoor areas, at the same time keeping out wind and rain. The geometry of the roof was inspired by the angles of the adjacent bridges and is a standardised steel structure like a big railway shed. A transport system over the river from the North Bank to the South Bank is also a part of the scheme – to link the buildings to the matrix of the city itself via pedestrian and vehicular links.

Client **South Bank Centre**

Architect **Richard Rogers Partnership**

Structural and Services Engineer **Ove Arup & Partners**

Quantity Surveyor **Davis Langdon & Everest**

Pedestrian Movement **Bartlett, University College of London**

Landscape Architect **Edward Hutchinson**

Computer Illustrations **Hayes Davidson**

Cost **£ 80m (at December 1995 prices)**

Programme **1994–2001**

Michael Wilford and Partners

Lowry Centre, Salford

The Lowry Centre will accommodate facilities for both
visual and performing arts to provide an exciting, stimulating venue for recreation and education. Bordered by
the Manchester Ship Canal and facing a new triangular
public plaza, it will be the landmark focus of the
redevelopment of Salford Quays. A hotel and multi-
storey car-park enclose the remaining sides and water-
side promenades provide pedestrian routes to the quays.

The building contains the 1,650-seat Lyric theatre, a
400-seat flexible theatre with rehearsal and dressing
facilities, art galleries to display the city's collection of
L. S. Lowry paintings, as well as changing exhibitions, a
Children's Gallery, together with bars, café and waterfront restaurant. Upper level bars on either side of the
Lyric theatre open onto roof terraces above the foyer
with views across the plaza.

As the workplace for a wide variety of people, the layout
of the building will encourage a sense of artistic community, and the administration tower is crowned by an
illuminated sign announcing current productions on
the Salford skyline.

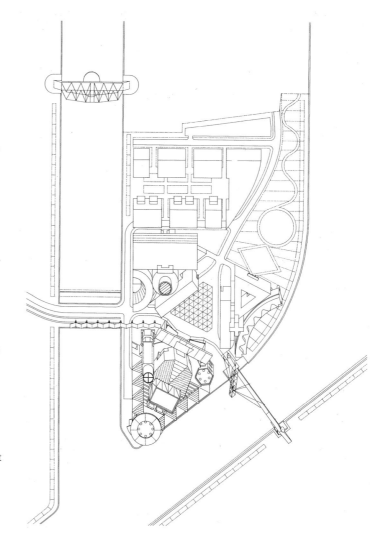

Client **Lowry Centre Trustees and City of Salford**

Architect **Michael Wilford and Partners Ltd.**

Project Manager **Gleeds Management Services**

Theatre Consultant **Theatre Projects Consultants**

Museum Consultant **Lord Cultural Resources**

Management Contractor **Bovis Construction Ltd.**

Acoustics Consultant **Sandy Brown Associates**

Structural, Mechanical and Electrical Engineers **Buro Happold**

Quantity Surveyor **Davis Langdon & Everest**

Childrens Gallery **Land Design**

Photography **Chris Edgecombe**

Cost **£50m**

Programme **1992–2000**

Colin St John Wilson and Partners

The British Library, St Pancras, London

The new British Library building replaces the existing British Library, which currently forms part of the British Museum complex in Bloomsbury. It houses the national collection of books, manuscripts, maps and patents as well as exhibition galleries, conservation laboratories, offices and lecture rooms.

The building provides for two very different main patterns of use: the humanities section features closed-access reading rooms in which readers are supplied with books from the storage basement; the science and patent section contains an open-access collection, and readers are able to find publications, abstracts and microfiches for themselves. Between these two sections lies the main entrance hall from which access to the public areas is possible. The main feature in the entrance hall is a six-floor-high bronze and glass tower housing the famous King's Library. There are three exhibition galleries open to the general public. The courtyard is the only large open space in the vicinity. When the Channel Tunnel Terminal is relocated to St Pancras, it will take on the status of one of London's major meeting points in addition to its role for events (or relaxation) in the Library. It is enclosed to the east by a conference centre which has its own separate entrance independent of the Library itself.

Client **The British Library (user);**
The Department of National Heritage (sponsor)
Architect **Colin St John Wilson & Partners Ltd.**
Structural Engineer **Ove Arup & Partners**
Services Engineer **Steensen Varming & Mulcahy**
Main Contractor **Laing Management**
Photography **John Donat**
Programme **1983–97**

Arup Associates
Plantation Place, London

Foster and Partners
Commerzbank Headquarters, Frankfurt

Foster and Partners
Millennium Tower, London

Nicholas Grimshaw and Partners
Berlin Stock Exchange and Chamber of Commerce

Sauerbruch Hutton Architects
GSW Headquarters, Berlin

Sir James Stirling and Michael Wilford and Partners
No. 1 Poultry, London

Commerce – The Work
Environment

More than any other building type, the office has been transformed over the last decade. The British design and construction industry has played a major role in this evolution, creating a new working environment that is more flexible, efficient and environmentally responsive than its predecessors. The concrete office slab of the 1960s, with cellular offices and small windows, has been replaced by generous open floors that enjoy daylight and transparency. The closed world of the office worker has become more accessible, creating a more integrated environment that blurs the edges between work and city living.

The needs of modern communications technology have been accommodated by new building technologies with adaptable raised floors, integrated suspended ceilings and computerised building control mechanisms. The office has become the experimental ground for the 'intelligent' building – one that measures the requirements of its users and responds with appropriate 'actions'. Shading devices open and close in response to solar exposure. Humidity and temperature controls are triggered automatically according to the number of occupants in any particular part of the building. And, natural systems of environmental control, air plenum, natural ventilation and flue effects, are replacing the need for energy intensive and ecologically damaging air conditioning systems.

But innovation is not only at the level of environmental services. The architectural form of the contemporary office building is changing in response to environmental pressures. Buildings are no longer designed to be the same on all sides but to respond directly to the different conditions of exposure and orientation. Optimisation of solar exposure (more natural light, better working conditions, less artificial light, less energy consumption), and reduction of heat loss, (more stable internal environment, lower heat load requirements, less energy consumption) are the fundamental design generators of Michael Hopkins' Inland Revenue Headquarters and Feilden Clegg's Building Research Establishment. In these build-

ings, the vertical flues, a late 20th-century interpretation of the 19th-century industrial chimney, play an important role in the architectural composition and environmental performance of the building. Norman Foster's Commerzbank and Millennium Tower have hanging gardens and sky lobbies on their south-facing facades, providing users with a 'window to the sky' that contributes to the environmental equilibrium of these vertical communities.

The economic argument for this change is compelling. Maintenance and running costs of office buildings quickly overtake capital building costs as the major expenditure in a building's lifespan. Many of the technical and design advantages currently being pioneered by British architects and engineers can reduce energy consumption, and hence expenditure, by at least 40%. In this respect, the office building is at the cutting edge of integrated design.

Many of the buildings in this section display spatial themes that are common to the emerging generation of British office and commercial buildings: strong street presence and identity (the late James Stirling's No. 1 Poultry), generous foyer and lobby spaces (Arup Associates' Plantation House) and the ubiquitous top-lit, glazed atrium (Nicholas Grimshaw's Berlin Stock Exchange and Terry Farrell's Samsung Headquarters). These architectural devices are not simply formal gestures. They are instrumental social mechanisms that foster a degree of interaction and cohesion between office workers and visitors and also play a fundamental role in the environmental performance of the building.

It is intriguing that this level of innovation in design has occurred despite a deeply conservative or traditional attitude to urbanism that has often stifled development and growth. Some of the more ambitious proposals for high-rise buildings in London, including Santiago Calatrava's City Point Tower and Norman Foster's Millennium Tower may never be realised in their original form and

The proposed development will create a new precinct in the City with three office buildings, shops, cafés and public performance areas. The curved, stepped shape of the central building is designed to be in scale with the street and the skyline. The tall building's impact on the streetscape is mitigated by perimeter buildings which respect the scale, height and character of the location. Light and reflection are key components in the design.

The design pays specific regard to the setting of the listed buildings at St Margaret Pattens Church and 43 Eastcheap nearby. The prominence of the church tower will be enhanced and its role as an historic local landmark greatly increased. The fabric of the church will be restored and new pedestrian routes into the site, along the currently inaccessible side and rear of the church, will enhance public perception of the City's heritage.

Client **British Land Company plc**

Architect, Structural Engineer and M&E Services Engineer

Arup Associates

CAD Image **Miller Hare**

Models **Millennium Models**

Photography **Simon Haregrove**

Foster and Partners

Commerzbank Headquarters, Frankfurt

This building is the world's highest ecological, symbolically and functionally 'green' structure. Its form is triangular, made up of three 'petals' and a central stem; the petals are the office floors, the stem a great central atrium which provides a natural ventilation chimney for the inward-looking offices. Four-storey-high gardens spiral around the triangular plan giving a view of the greenery from each workplace and eliminating large expanses of unbroken office space. Lifts, stairs and services are placed in groups to reinforce the village-like clusters of offices and gardens. Pairs of vertical masts, enclosing the corner cores, support eight-storey vierendeel beams, which in turn support clear span office floors; thus both offices and gardens are free of structural elements.

The city block containing the new fifty-three-storey tower is opened up with a new public space, a winter-garden housing restaurants, cafés and space for performances and exhibitions of works of art. The perimeter buildings contain a rich mix of apartments, shops, banks and car parking, as well as a new auditorium for the Bank. The tower is curently the tallest in Europe at over 300 metres (984 ft.).

Client **Commerzbank AG**

Architect **Foster and Partners**

Structural Engineer **Ove Arup & Partners with Krebs & Kiefer**

M&E Services Engineer **J. Roger Preston & Partners with Pettersen & Ahrends**

Quantity Surveyor **Davis Langdon & Everest**

Electrical Engineer **Schad und Hölzel**

Transport Systems **Jappsen und Stangier**

Project Management **Nervus GmbH**

Space Planning **Quickborner Team**

Lighting **Claude Engle**

Landscape **Sommerlad und Partner**

Graphics **Per Arnoldi**

Photography **Richard Davies, Ian Lambert**

Programme **1994–97**

Foster and Partners

Millennium Tower, London

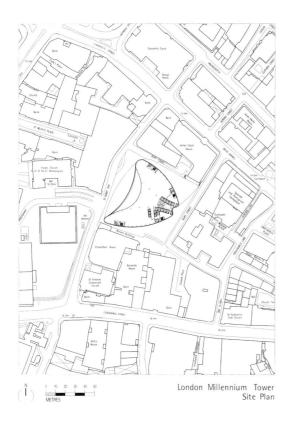

London Millennium Tower
Site Plan

The London Millennium Tower, a ninety-two-storey office structure, was proposed for the site of the Baltic Exchange, which was badly damaged by an IRA bomb in 1992.

At 1,265 ft (plus its mast), the building would have been taller than both the main tower at Canary Wharf (880 ft), at present the highest office building in Britain, and Europe's tallest tower, the new Commerzbank head-quarters in Frankfurt (984 ft), also designed by Foster and Partners.

With a curved free-form plan, the building's appearance constantly changes as different qualities of sunlight hit the continuous curves of the glass facade. The top of the building divides into two elegant tail fins of different heights allowing every view of the building to be unique. The London Millennium Tower, with some 1.5 million sq. ft of usable space, provides prestige offices, dealing floors, apartments, shops, restaurants, cafés and gardens in the sky. There is a public viewing gallery with breath-taking panoramic views of London in the large glass atrium at exactly 1,000 ft.

The site is free from many of the constraints which normally limit the scale of development in the City of London. It is not a conservation area and is unaffected by height limits imposed on buildings closer to St Paul's Cathedral. It lies within an existing cluster of high-rise buildings which include the Lloyds Building, the Commercial Union Tower, and the Natwest Tower. Never-theless planning permission was refused, and Foster and Partners were asked to prepare a smaller design.

156

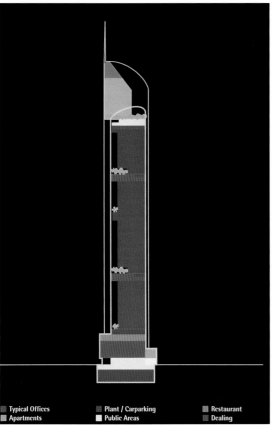

Typical Offices   Plant / Carparking   Restaurant
Apartments   Public Areas   Dealing

Client **London Millennium Tower Ltd (a subsidiary of Kværner)**

Architect **Foster and Partners**

Structural Engineer **Ove Arup & Partners**

M&E Services Engineer **FC Foreman & Partners;**
Roger Preston & Partners

Quantity Surveyor **Franklin & Andrews**

Development Consultants **BHZ; Jones Lang Wootton**

Planning Consultants **Grimley**

Cladding Consultants **Emmer Pfenniger & Partner**

Lift Consultants **Lerch Bates & Associates**

Photography **Tom Miller (montage), Richard Davies**

Programme **1996 (design)**

Nicholas Grimshaw and Partners

Berlin Stock Exchange and Chamber of Commerce

The brief called for the fusing of the Chamber of Commerce with the Berlin Stock Exchange into a single 'Communication Centre', together with lettable office suites, a conference centre and catering facilities.

The design is based on three precepts: firstly, that it should be built right up to the irregular rear site boundary to avoid a tall building; secondly, that there should be a rapport between the scheme's internal life and that of the city; and, thirdly, that its public functions should be arrayed along an inner 'street'.

The upper floors are suspended from fifteen elliptical arches of depths varying in accordance with the rear boundary, thus giving complete design freedom by eliminating columns, and making the ground floor lighter and more open. Office accommodation is organised around a pair of three-sided, unheated atria that moderate the harsh Berlin continental climate and bring daylight to the heart of this deep plan. Although atria floors are one level up from the inner street, these spaces are linked, creating spectacular surprise views through the depths of the building.

Client **Berlin Chamber of Commerce and Industry; Berlin Association of Merchants and Industrialists**
Architect **Nicholas Grimshaw and Partners**
Structural Engineer **Whitby & Bird**
M&E Services Engineer **RP & K Sozietät**
Quantity Surveyor **Davis Langdon & Everest; Mott Green & Wall (Services)**
Project Manager **Buro 4/SMV**
Contractor **Michael Weiss & Partners**
Photography Images **Nicholas Grimshaw and Partners**
Cost **£66m**
Programme **1991 (competition) 1994–98**

Sauerbruch Hutton Architects

GSW Headquarters, Berlin

This design forms the extension to an office tower which was built as one of the first reconstruction projects in the Berlin of the 1950s. The scheme combines clearly defined volumes, including the existing tower, as fragments of urbanity into a new three-dimensional composition. The idea of conglomerate growth is not only accepted, but put forward as a model for urban development. The new ensemble reacts as much to the baroque logic of the plan as it responds to the rules of 19th-century urbanism; it absorbs the object-quality of the 1950s tower and registers the existing confrontational space across the Berlin Wall.

In this combination of the disparate spatial configurations from consecutive generations, the new high-rise is the element associated with the present and the future. Its design is generated by a concern for the workplace in the city, and by an interest for an architecture economical with the (built and natural) resources of the environment. The result is a building that offers an exemplary working environment which controls its energy consumption through the 'passive' means of its architecture.

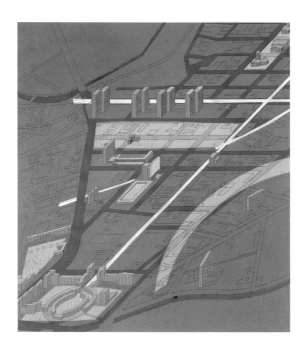

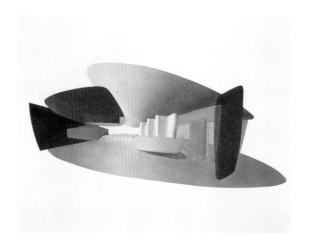

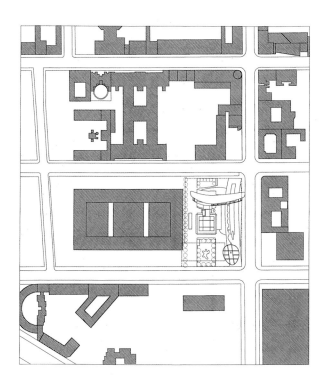

Client **Gemeinnützige Siedlungs- und Wohnungsbau-Gesellschaft mbH**

Architect **Sauerbruch Hutton Architects**

Structural Engineer **Ove Arup & Partners/IGH**

M&E Services Engineer **IGH/Ove Arup & Partners**

Quantity Surveyor **Harms & Partner**

Contractor **Züblin, Götz**

Photography **Lepkowski & Hillman Studios, Uwe Rau**

Cost DM **130m**

Programme **March 1995–April 1999**

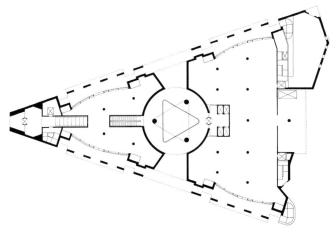

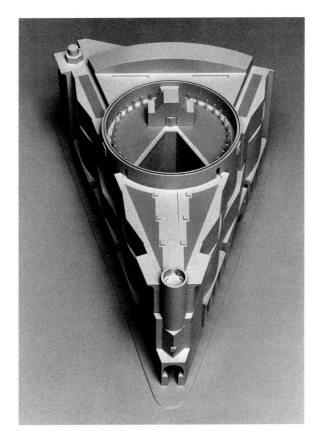

No. 1 Poultry is planned about a central longitudinal axis with similar facades to Queen Victoria Street and Poultry. The design was determined by the existing informal street pattern and the surrounding historic buildings. The parapet height and vertical division of the facades into distinct parts also correspond to surrounding buildings. The new building contains shops at basement and ground levels, with five floors of offices, a roof garden and restaurant above. A pedestrian passage through the building provides a link to an open courtyard which brings daylight into the centre of the building and to the shopping levels. The courtyard, with interlocking circular and triangular plans, extends to the basement shopping area and Bank Underground Station.

Public access to the offices is from the courtyard, with a ceremonial entrance from the apex of the building via a grand stairway to the first-floor balcony of the courtyard. The centre of the garden is enclosed by a circular pergola around the courtyard, forming a sanctuary from the bustle of the city. The building is faced in sandstone and granite with bronze metalwork.

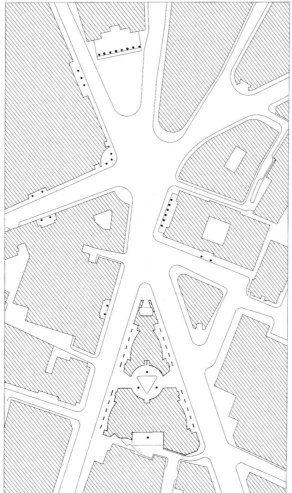

Client **City Acre Property Investment Trust and Altstadtbau Ltd.**
Architect **Sir James Stirling and Michael Wilford and Partners Ltd.**
Structural, Mechanical and Electrical Engineers **Ove Arup & Partners**
Quantity Surveyor **Monk Dunstone Associates**
Landscape **Lennox-Boyd Landscape Design Ltd.**
Planning Agents **Montagu Evans**
Architects for site **Armstrong Smith and Baron**
Facades **Arup Facade Engineering**
Contractor **John Laing Construction Ltd.**
Photography **John Donat**
Cost **£40m**
Programme **1985–97**

Terry Farrell and Partners
International Centre for Life, Newcastle-upon-Tyne

Feilden Clegg Architects, New Environmental Office,
Building Research Establishment (BRE), Garston

Future Systems
The Ark Earth Centre, Doncaster

Nicholas Grimshaw & Partners
Eden Project, St Austell, Cornwall

Michael Hopkins and Partners
The Inland Revenue Centre, Nottingham

David Marks Julia Barfield Architects
Weather-Watch Discovery Centre, Bracknell

Stanton Williams
Millennium Seed Bank, Kew Gardens, London

Studio E
Solar Office, Doxford International, Sunderland

Ecology

Environmental performance has become a key generator of architectural form. This is a growing international trend that recognises the importance buildings play in the global environmental equation. It is estimated that well-designed buildings can help reduce energy consumption (and, in turn, pollution) by at least 40%, contributing to substantial savings in environmental and running costs. Public and commercial organisations alike, as well as the typical domestic user, recognise the long-term benefits of energy-efficient buildings that provide a sustainable solution to future needs.

Over the last decade, British architects and engineers have successfully combined their skills and knowledge, leading to a number of significant developments in energy-conscious design. These developments are at the forefront of interdisciplinary design innovation, and have become widely used at an international scale. They include heat-sensitive building 'skins' that respond to changes in external conditions, improved insulation techniques, employment of non-renewable sources of energy such as solar and wind power, and, the use of masonry structure as thermal mass to store and conserve energy. Together they constitute the state-of-the-art of building services engineering and sustainable architectural design.

The common concern that drives innovation in building design is the need to conserve energy. This can be achieved by working with the natural environment rather than against it. Many buildings featured in the exhibition are designed around simple – yet radical – environmental concepts: maximising natural ventilation; reducing solar gain and heat loss, and using renewable sources of energy and non-polluting materials and services.

Optimisation of solar exposure (more natural light, better working conditions, less artificial light, less energy consumption) and reduction of heat loss (more stable internal environment, lower heat load requirements, less energy consumption) are the fundamental design generators of Michael Hopkins' Inland Revenue Headquarters. The round towers double up as architectural statements and as vertical flues with opening umbrellas that encourage air movement to cool the buildings in summer. Vertical flues, a late 20th-century interpretation of the 19th-century industrial chimney, play an equally important role in the architectural composition and environmental performance of Feilden Clegg's Building Research Establishment, a design that integrates advanced systems of environmental technology and control.

Apart from enclosing every known plant species in the world's largest greenhouse, Nicholas Grimshaw's cascading glass Eden Centre is a highly sophisticated example of environmental control of a vast covered space. Future System's Earth Centre at Doncaster and Terry Farrell's Centre for Life employ organic forms and responsive materials (heat responsive glass, photo-voltaics and natural ventilation) to enhance the environmental performance of the building. Many of these projects belong to the current generation of buildings that is far more responsive to climate and environmental context than their modernist or post-modernist predecessors.

Terry Farrell and Partners

International Centre for Life, Newcastle-upon-Tyne

The £ 54 million International Centre for Life located next to Central Station on a prominent site at the Western Gateway to Newcastle Upon Tyne, is one of the fourteen landmark millennium projects situated across the United Kingdom.

The International Centre for Life contains four main elements: HELIX, a 9100 sq.m. futuristic and interactive, themed, indoor, family entertainment centre accommodating up to 300,000 visitors per year. HELIX will explore DNA, how it works, and what it means for humans; the Genetics Institute, 5,400 sq.m. of accommodation for the North East's world class, human genetics research group comprising over 150 academic and specialist clinical consulting service staff. The Genetics Institute will provide clinical applications for research and act as a major centre for research into inherited diseases such as cystic fibrosis and muscular dystrophy, infectious diseases, cancer and heart disease; the Bio Science Centre providing 8000 sq.m. of specialist commercial laboratory and office space for small to medium size companies engaged in biotechnology; and a further 2,000 sq.m. of retail accommodation.

The architectural design approach is based on a collage of ideas and built forms that eschews any one singular design approach. The most powerful visual image of HELIX is the wave form roof over the entrance and daylit part of the exhibition galleries and education facilities. The main galleries are a flexible serviced "black box" providing large volume, clear span areas for themed exhibitions. The range of materials used in the construction of the HELIX centre include timber, render, pre-patinated copper roofing, profile metal cladding and curtain walling. A variable message media wall facing the main railway lines announces the scheme to people arriving in or passing through Newcastle, whilst a sky-sign and double helix sculpture firmly establish the design on the Newcastle skyline.

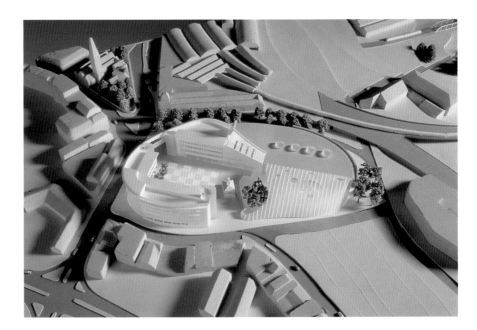

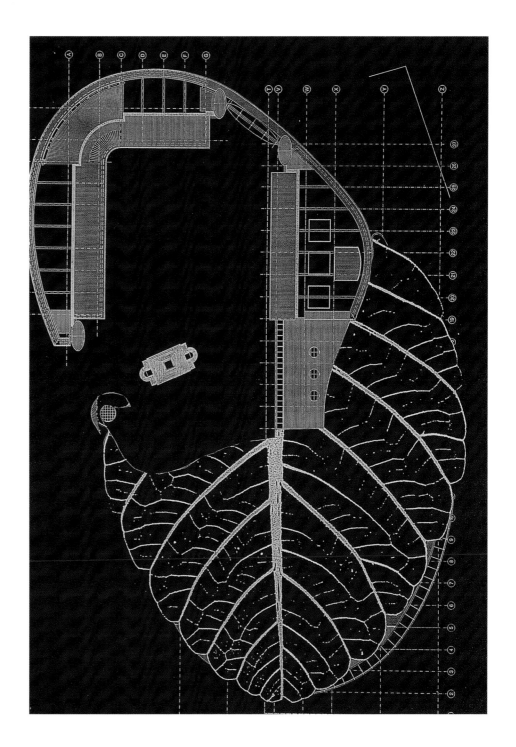

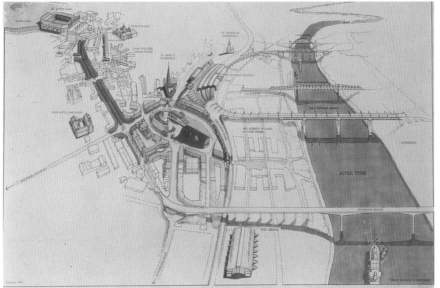

Client **Tyne & Wear Development Corporation/ICL Trust**
Architect **Terry Farrell and Partners**
Structural and Services Engineer **Mott MacDonald**
Exhibition Designer **Event Communications Ltd.**
Quantity Surveyor **Gardiner & Theobald**
Contractor **John Laing Construction Ltd.**
Landscape Architect **Gillespies**
Models **Terry Farrell & Partners – Study Model, Unit 2:2**
Photography **Terry Farrell & Partners, Andrew Putler**
(study model)
Cost **£54m**
Programme **Completion: Easter 2000**

Feilden Clegg Architects

New Environmental Office, Building Research Establishment (BRE), Garston

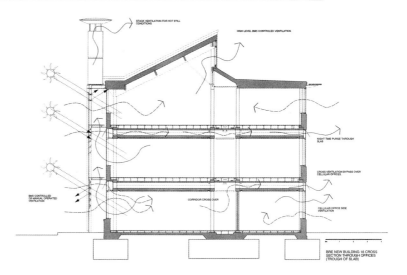

The design is a landmark office building for 100 people at the heart of BRE's campus at Garston. The offices were to be designed to a performance specification devised as part of the 'Energy Efficient Office of the Future' project, a partnership between BRE and the construction industry, investigating the parameters of low-energy, comfortable and healthy workplaces for the twenty-first century. This building is the first of a number of demonstration projects for different locations.

Some of the energy-efficient design features are as follows: wave-form, exposed structural concrete slab incorporating bore hole cooling; highly-glazed facades with external glass louvres and controlled artificial lighting; solar and fan-assisted ventilation stacks; extensive use of recycled materials; and, enough photo-voltaic panels to light the building.

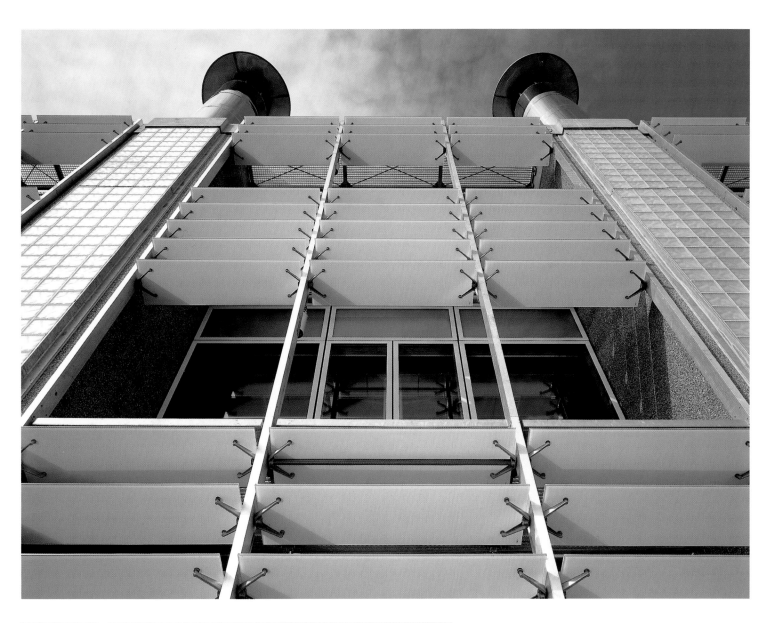

Client **Building Research Establishment Ltd**
Architect **Feilden Clegg Architects**
Structural Engineer **Buro Happold**
Quantity Surveyor **Turner & Townsend**
Project Management **BWA Project Services**
Environmental Services Engineer **Max Fordham & Partners**
Landscape Architect **Nicholas Pearson Associates**
Planning Supervisor **Symonds Travers Morgan Ltd**
Main Contractor **J. Sisk & Son Ltd**
Photographer **Dennis Gilbert/View**
Cost **£2.9m**
Programme **1994–95 (designed), 1995–96 (constructed)**

Future Systems

The Ark Earth Centre, Doncaster

The Ark Earth Centre is a vast, lightweight exhibition hall housing a wide range of exciting, multi-media exhibits and auditoria, highlighting the critical environmental issues of our time. The design aims to express the ideals of a humanity that respects nature and an enhanced quality of life, and an architecture that is soft and organic to enclose the energy-efficient, non-polluting technologies of the twenty-first century.

The building is conceived as a brightly-coloured, hovering butterfly-like form, creating harmony with the newly-restored landscape. The roof creates a single span under which the various exhibits are arranged on three free-form floors connected by escalators, permitting easy circulation. The multi-coloured roof surface is a living, breathing skin of energy-generating photo-voltaic panels. Sheer glass along the front of the building signals the entrance, drawing in people from around the park, and a telecommunications mast provides a symbolic focus as well as a beacon of light that can be seen for miles. At night, the building glows from within, emitting a romantic coloured light.

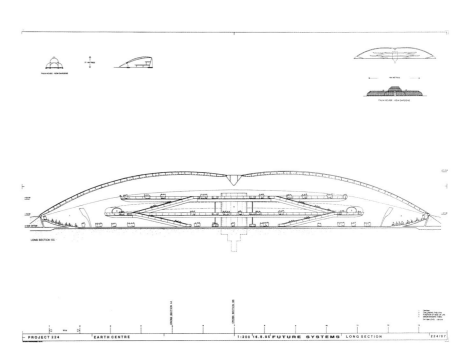

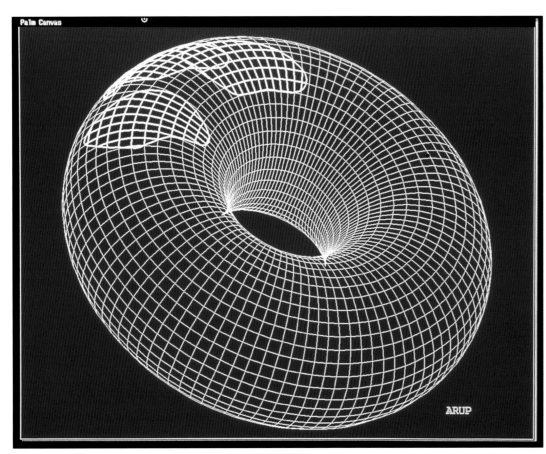

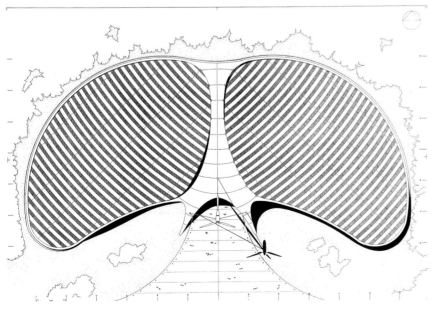

Client **The Earth Centre**

Architect **Future Systems**

Structural and Environmental Engineer **Ove Arup & Partners**

Quantity Surveyor **Bernard Williams Associates**

Cost **£15m**

Photography Image **Future Systems**

Programme **Completion 2000**

Nicholas Grimshaw & Partners

The Eden Project, St Austell, Cornwall

The Eden Project will be a showcase for global bio-diversity and human dependence upon plants. There will be 2.6 hectare of linked, climate-controlled transparent capsules (biomes) set in a designed landscape, accessed via a visitor centre where visitors will experience the world of plants using micro and time-lapse photography.

The biomes will encapsulate three key climatological regions: rain forest, sub-tropics and Mediterranean temperate. A clear distinction has been made between the interior and exterior by structuring the building as an exoskeleton, with a soft clear membrane suspended beneath the lightweight, taut steel structure. Over the last few months the biome structural system has evolved from a series of trusses interconnected by secondary beams into a dome system. The geometry of the domes enables a very lightweight structure of minimal surface and maximum volume to be created; this helps with fabrication, transportation and erection techniques.

The system consists of straight tubular compressive members connected by standard cast connections. These create a primary geometry consisting of hexagonal cells spanning roughly nine metres across. The cladding system which is made up of optically clear air inflated foil 'pillows' provides one of the most transparent envelopes ever designed. Once the principle for a single dome was established, they generated the complete biomes by inserting further domes of differing diameters, creating the impression of groups of soap bubbles. As the site is also a clay pit which is still in use, the domes can be adjusted to meet any changes in ground level between now and when construction commences.

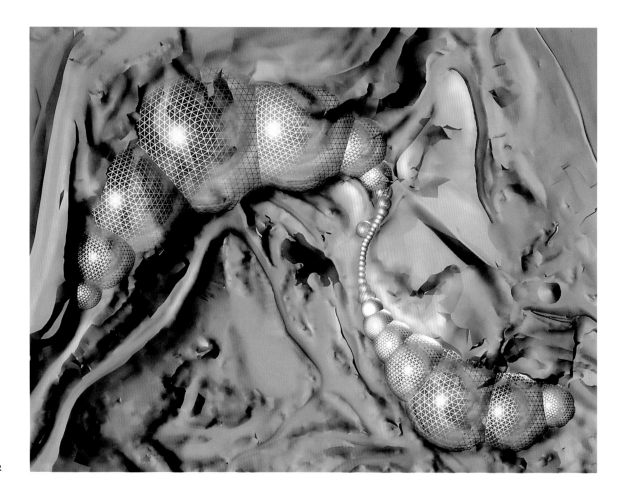

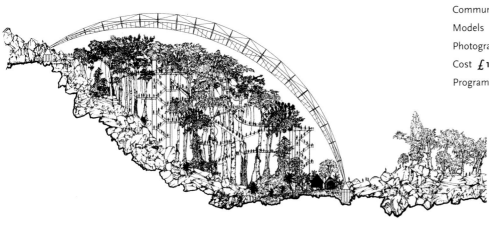

Client **The Eden Trust**
Architect **Nicholas Grimshaw & Partners**
Structural Engineer **Anthony Hunt Associates**
Environmental Engineer, Economics and Planning
Ove Arup & Partners
Quantity Surveyor **Davis Langdon & Everest**
Landscape Architect **Land Use Consultants**
Project Managers **Davis Langdon & Everest**
Communications and Design **Imagination**
Models **Andrew Ingham Associates**
Photography **Michael Dyer Associates**
Cost £106m (Phase 1 – £70m)
Programme 1997–Easter 2000

Michael Hopkins and Partners

The Inland Revenue Centre, Nottingham

The new development is bounded by a canal to the north and a railway line to the south. The three- and four-storey office buildings form traditional city blocks enclosing gardens, and are designed to control the internal environment by passive means. The office wings are only 13.6m deep to best use natural light and ventilation; also maximum use is made of daylight via 'light shelves' over the windows.

The central circulation route is offset to allow both cellular and open-plan accommodation, with glazed cylindrical stair towers signalling the entrance to each block. Warm air is drawn from the office areas into the towers and travels up the open stairwell to roof vents. There is no air conditioning and heating is by low-pressure hot-water radiators. In order to achieve the high thermal mass required by the passive environmental design, construction is mainly of heavy materials. Precast concrete floor units act as a folded plate and span the full width of the blocks. The floor plates sit on load-bearing piers of Nottingham semi-engineering brick which reduce in section as the load diminishes on the upper levels. Steel trusses support a roof of lead-clad plywood panels reflecting the adjacent Victorian brick buildings with dark grey roofs.

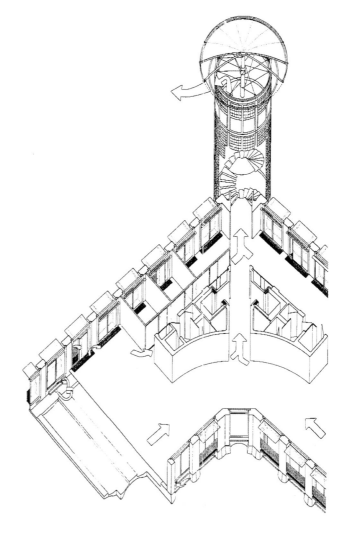

Client **Inland Revenue, Nottingham**
Client Project Manager **Turner & Townsend Project Management**
Architect **Michael Hopkins and Partners**
Structural Engineer **Ove Arup & Partners**
Quantity Surveyor **Turner & Townsend**
Management Contractor **Laing Management**
Acoustic Consultant **Arup Acoustics**
Photography **Dennis Gilbert**
Programme **1992–94**

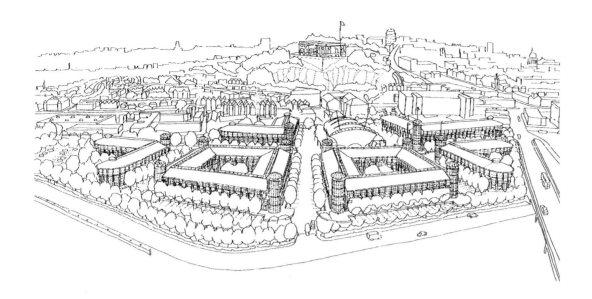

David Marks Julia Barfield Architects

Weather-Watch Discovery Centre, Bracknell

The Weather-Watch Discovery Centre has been designed as a focus for education, information and debate in response to a growth in public interest in meteorology. It will provide a dramatic new symbol for Bracknell, home of the Meteorological Office.

The project consists of two elements: An eighty-metre high stainless steel tower containing petals of dichroic glass which responds to the natural rhythms of wind and light, a high-quality interactive children's discovery centre which will describe in an educational and entertaining way the forces shaping weather and climate, and the technologies used to understand and predict them.

The tower is designed as a guyed mast, in effect a triangular truss with beams made from three circular hollow sections. The horizontal hoops and the diagonal rods providing the bracing and bending in the mast are controlled by pre-stressing the guys. Fluctuations in wind and light will be reflected in, and transmitted through 'petals' of dichroic glass which will be suspended within the shaft of the polished stainless steel tower. The 'petals' will be constrained on two opposite corners by purpose-made stainless steel hinges, thus allowing them to almost free-fly to shed load.

The Discovery Centre will have a smooth aerodynamic shell structure to minimise undesirable local wind effects, and a low surface area: volume ratio reduces heat loss. Its highly reflective surface of stainless steel and glass provides excellent solar control which, combined with the shape of the interior, enable the building to be nearly entirely naturally ventilated. A glass enclosure over part of the structure will allow visitors to look up at the ever-changing tower above.

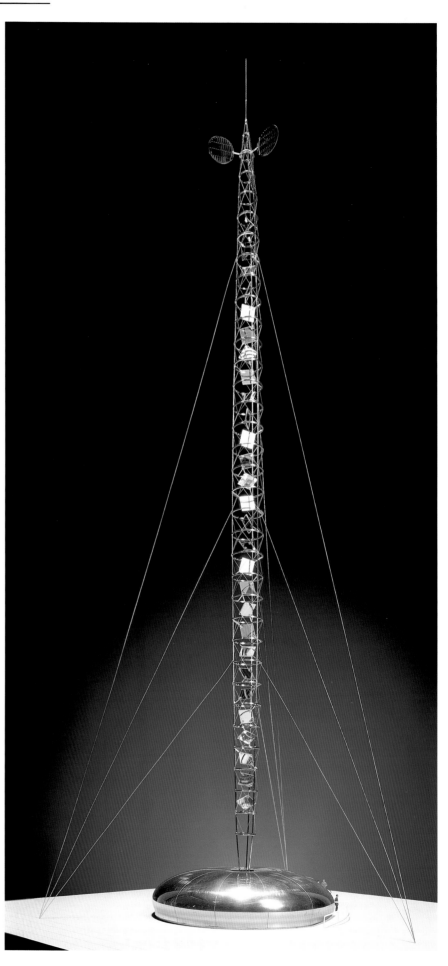

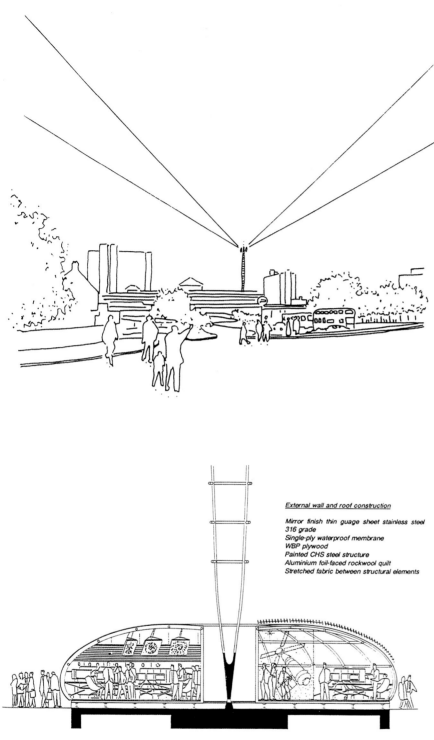

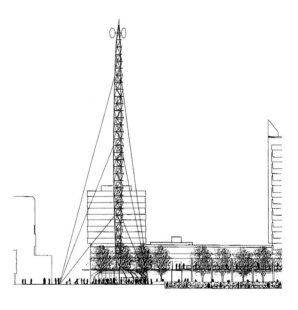

External wall and roof construction

Mirror finish thin guage sheet stainless steel
316 grade
Single-ply waterproof membrane
WBP plywood
Painted CHS steel structure
Aluminium foil-faced rockwool quilt
Stretched fabric between structural elements

Internal wall construction

Plasterboard on 6mm plywood on metal stud

Floor construction

Heavy duty linoleum on screed
Raised floor of precast concrete planks on brick bearing stub walls
Concrete raft

Client **Bracknell Forest Borough Council**
Architect **David Marks Julia Barfield Architects**
Structural Engineer **Ove Arup & Partners**
Project Manager **Technology Response Ltd.**
Quantity Surveyor **Gardiner & Theobald**
Lanscape Architect **Edward Hutchison Landscape Architects**
Models **WED**
Photography **Graham Challifour**

Stanton Williams

Millennium Seed Bank, Kew Gardens, London

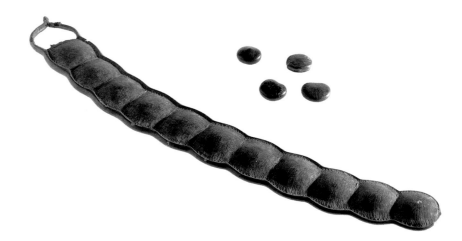

The project's aim is the conservation of seed samples from 25,000 species by the year 2010, including all of the UK flora by the year 2000. The facility will be available for the safe deposit of seeds from many sources, in particular the world's dryland where human welfare is absolutely dependant upon plants. The overall building form will be coherent and simple. Whilst it will have its own identity as a significant research and archive establishment, it must also fit into the existing village of residential and agricultural buildings situated in an area of outstanding natural beauty. The design aims to create a sequence of flexible research spaces, and a public winter-garden that should both inspire and focus the mind on the importance of seed collection.

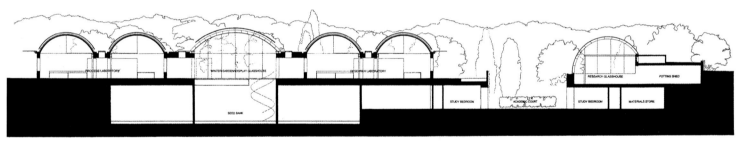

Client **Royal Britannic Gardens, Kew**

Architect **Stanton Williams**

Structural Engineer **Michael Barclay Partnership**

Quantity Surveyor **Gordon Fanshawe and Partners**

M&E Services Engineer **Pearce Buckle Partnership**

Environmental Consultants **EA Planning**

Models **James Wink**

Photography **Stanton Williams**

Cost **£10.5m**

Programme **Completion 1999**

Studio E

Solar Office, Doxford International, Sunderland

The Solar Office is the first speculatively constructed office building anywhere to incorporate building-integrated photo-voltaics and the resulting solar facade is the largest so far constructed. The building is designed to minimise the use of energy while its extended fabric is designed to replace such energy as is used. This formula for energy self-sufficiency is one of the key building blocks of future global sustainability. The plan is V-shaped with the extreme ends of the V splayed away from each other; a central core is located at the apex. The building incorporates a sixty-six-metre-long, south-facing atrium and, between the facade and the splayed wings, an internal 'street'.

The facade was aligned to face due south and sloped at 60° to the ground, thus maximising solar radiation; the sealed and inclined facade overcame the potential problem of dazzle and provided an effective barrier to noise from passing traffic. By placing the car park in front of the building, it ensured that the solar facade would not be over-shadowed and that a sense of anticipation would be felt by revealing the facade only after encircling the building.

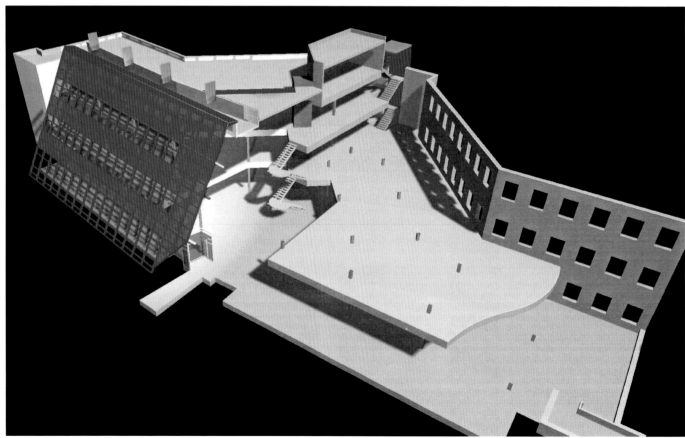

Client **Akeler Developments plc**

Architect **Studio E**

Co-ordinating Architect **Aukett Associates**

Structural Engineer **Whitby & Bird**

Building Services **Rybka Battle**

Contractor **Bowmer & Kirkland**

Photography **Simon Hazelgrove**

Cost **£4.5m**

Programme **1997–98**

Biographies

Ahrends Burton and Koralek was established by Peter Ahrends, Richard Burton and Paul Koralek in 1961 after Koralek won the international competition for the New Library in Trinity College Dublin. They have since won numerous awards for design and technical achievement with projects in the UK, Ireland and Europe. The practice achieved notoriety for its modernist credentials when their competition-winning scheme for the extension of the National Gallery in London was described by the Prince of Wales as "a carbuncle on the face of a dear friend", leading to its rejection. ABK has since recovered from the blow, and more recent projects range from the energy-saving St Mary's Hospital on the Isle of Wight, to eleven stations for the Dock-lands Light Railway in London, the new British Embassy in Moscow, a learning resource centre for Selly Oak Colleges, departmental buildings at Loughborough University, and ex-tensions to Manchester's Whitworth Gallery. The practice also has an office in Dublin.

Allies and Morrison was established in 1984 by Bob Allies and Graham Morrison who met in 1978 while working in the office of Martin Richardson. They formed the practice following their success in the competition to re-design the public space at the Mound, Edinburgh. Since then, they have established their reputation as purveyors of a restrained, Scandinavian-inspired modernism through a series of relatively small-scale domestic and educational projects; such as Morrison's own house in Blackheath and Sarum Hall School in North London; and, more recently, larger schemes such as the new building for Newnham College, Cambridge, and the British Embassy in Dublin. Both Allies and Morrison have chosen to combine practice with teaching – Allies at Cambridge and Edinburgh, and now Bath University, Morrison at North East London Polytechnic up until 1991 when he was elected on to join the RIBA Council. He chaired the exhibition committee from 1992–94 and helped establish the RIBA Architecture Centre. He is a director of the RIBA Journal and is a member of the Arts Council architectural advisory panel.

Alsop & Störmer Architects has offices in London, Hamburg, Moscow and Hong Kong. William Alsop trained at the Architec-tural Association and he originally established a practice with John Lyall, (Alsop and Lyall), which became known for its ex-uberant approach to architecture, characterised by the use of unusual shapes and forms and vivid colour in a growing number of controversial projects. The sausage-shaped Cardiff Bay Visitors Centre, which was originally intended as a temporary structure proved so popular it has become a permanent architectural feature of the Bay development area. It won an RIBA national award in 1991. The Regional Government headquarters in

Marseille, known locally as the "Big Blue", was the result of one of a series of fruitful collaborations with the artist Bruce McLean. Alsop's own paintings, which form an integral part of his design process, have been exhibited in the UK and Germany, and he is a fellow of the Royal Society of Arts as well as an honorary fellow of the Royal Society of British Sculptors. He has been a visiting professor in the United States, Australia, and Germany and is currently Professor of architecture at the University of Vienna. Projects in progress include: Blackfriars Thameslink 2000 Station, Peckham Library, North Greenwich Station in London and a Passenger and Ferry Terminal in Hamburg.

Armstrong Architects was established in London in 1986 by Kenneth and Jenifer Armstrong. Kenneth Armstrong trained at the Macintosh School, Glasgow and the Royal College of Art, and went on to work at Foster and Partners, where he met David Chipperfield with whom he originally set up practice. Jenifer Armstrong trained at the Bartlett School, London. Armstrong Architects work, including offices, shops, private residences, and urban masterplanning studies are often asso-ciated with the so-called "minimalist" tendency in architecture. Their work was featured in the 1990 exhibition at the 9H Gallery, entitled *Reality and Project: Four British Architects*. In 1991 Armstrong Architects rose to prominence by winning the international competition for the Maison du Japon in Paris, as a result of which the practice relocated to Paris. The building was completed earlier this year to considerable acclaim.

Arup Associates was founded in 1963 as a parallel partnership to engineers Ove Arup & Partners to provide architecture driven by an integrated design approach and dedicated to the develop-ment of new structural technology and a modernist aesthetic. It is a large, multi-disciplinary practice with a solid foundation in commercial work for the public and private sectors, including offices, hotels, conference centres, cultural and education build-ings, and large residential developments. By 1985 Arup Associates had received more RIBA awards than any other practice in England. Since then it has won the Fulton Award for excellence in use of concrete and the South African Association of Consulting engineers award for engineering excellence for its Johannesburg Athletics Stadium. It was 'Multidisciplinary Practice of the Year' in the 1997 Building awards, and won this year's London Region RIBA award for 3 The Square, Stockley Park.

Behnisch & Partner was established by Günter Behnisch in 1953. Since then thay have designed and supervised the construction of about one hundred and twenty buildings, and a further five to six hundred buildings were designed for architectural competitions. Over the last forty-four years the practice has undergone changes in response to the work that comes in the office. From 1968 to 1972, they set up an office to carry out the planning for the Munich Olympic Park. For some years now there have been two practices in Stuttgart, and a branch office in Lübeck in northern Germany. Some of their recent projects include the conversion to the Munich Olympic Park, a new control tower for Nuremberg Airport, a residential complex in Ingolstadt-Hollerstauden, the Centre for Performing Arts in Bristol, and the new Academy of Fine Arts in Berlin. This year they re-named the company Behnisch, Behnisch and Partners acknowledging the contribution of Stefan Behnisch.

Benson + Forsyth was founded in 1978 by Gordon Benson and Alan Forsyth, both of whom trained at the Architectural Association. The practice's built work started with a series of housing projects in the seventies which referred to a tradition of minimal modernism. This was followed by the Boarbank Oratory and Boarbank Hall Physiotherapy Room in 1986, and a pavilion at the Glasgow Garden Festival,1989. They consolidated their Scottish connections by winning the international competition for a new Museum of Scotland in Edinburgh, which is now under construction alongside a series of other cultural projects in Scotland and the north, including the Wordsworth Trust Library and the Century Theatre in Cumbria, and the Cowgatehead Library, Edinburgh. Gordon Benson is visiting professor at the University of Edinburgh. In Japan the practice has designed the Temple of Time/Divided House in Oshima, and the Jyonhanna Storehouse Museum.

Architekturbüro Bolles-Wilson is the partnership of German-born Julia B. Bolles-Wilson and Australian-born Peter Wilson, who met at the Architectural Association in London. The practice has been based in Münster since winning the commission for the new City Library in 1993. Projects for a technology centre followed and the WLV Office Building, also in Münster, and a kindergarten in Frankfurt which has been widely acclaimed. Their work is characterised by a thoughtful, highly-detailed approach and a concern for a high standard of craftsmanship which was first publicly demonstrated in the house and office designed for David and Janice Blackburn in North London. The somewhat introspective character and precision of the architectural conception is reflected in Wilson's immaculate and beautiful drawings. The shift to a bigger scale has prompted comparisons with northern European architects such as Scharoun and Aalto.

Branson Coates Architecture was formed in 1987, by Doug Branson and Nigel Coates with the stated objective of providing a multi-disciplinary approach to architectural design. Branson Coates initially become known for a series of projects in Japan, including Café Bongo and The Wall, at a time when its work was still regarded as too daring for British taste. They completed twenty projects in Japan, and a number of striking shop interiors in Britain, followed more recently by two public buildings currently on site: the National Centre of Popular Music, Sheffield, and the Geffrye Museum extension in east London. In the past two years Branson Coates has designed several exhibitions, including the Royal Academy's 'Living Bridges' exhibition, and the 'Power of Erotic Design' at the Design Museum in London. Other current commissions include the Gdansk Shakespearean Theatre, Poland, and the British Pavilion for Expos '98 and 2000. Both Doug Branson and Nigel Coates studied at the Architectural Association and Nigel Coates is Professor of Architecture at the Royal College of Art.

David Chipperfield Architects was founded in 1984, and initially built shops worldwide for Issey Miyake, Joseph, Equipment and Katharine Hamnett. The pared-down modern approach, combined with the richness of immaculately detailed natural materials, is inspired by Japanese aesthetics, and Chipperfield's first major new-build projects, a museum and an office headquarters, were built in Japan. In Britain the practice recently completed the Henley Rowing Museum, and has been shortlisted in many high-profile competitions, including the Bankside Tate and the Performing Arts Centre in Bristol. Current projects include, the Neues Museum in Berlin, the Cornerhouse Arts Centre in Manchester, and the Landeszentral Bank in Gera, Germany. The practice also continues to combine its architectural work with furniture design, and currently has three ranges in production in Japan and Italy.

CZWG was formed in 1975, formalising the partnership of Nick Campbell, Roger Zogolovitch (who has now retired as a partner), Rex Wilkinson and Piers Gough who had all trained together at the Architectural Association. Their early work quickly established the practice's flamboyant, humorous approach to architecture which has continued to be its distinguishing characteristic. Several of their projects included conversions, most notably the offices for Time Out and mixed commercial buildings at Gresse Street, London, which won an RICS/Times conservation award and a Civic Trust commendation. During the 1980s, CZWG became closely involved with the redevelopment of Docklands, realising a number of private housing schemes on both sides of the river, including China Wharf, The Circle, and Cascades. More recently, the practice completed a turquoise tile-clad public lavatory in Notting Hill, which attracted huge media interest and won the Royal Fine Art Commission Jeu d'Esprit award. On a rather larger scale, the practice has built two art, design and technology centres at Uppingham and Bryanston Schools, and an office scheme for Cochrane Square in Glasgow, and won the competition to masterplan a 43-acre site in the Gorbals, Glasgow.

Nick Derbyshire Design Associates was formed out of the former in-house design team of British Rail, which achieved a notable triumph with the reconstruction of Liverpool Street Station. Other recent work includes the design and construction supervision of Ashford international and domestic railway stations, the design of Moorgate Station for Crossrail, and the planning and design of St Pancras International Terminal for Union Railways. The practice's skills and ability to solve complex design, restoration and interchange issues have won it many awards, notably the Lord Montagu Trophy for Liverpool Street Station, and the Railway Heritage Trust Award for their restoration of Bury St Edmunds station.

ECD Architects was established in 1980 but, since 1995, has operated as two related companies – ECD Architects and ECD Energy & Environment – offering architectural, energy and environmental consultancy services. ECD Architects employs twenty-four staff including three working directors: David Turrent, Richard Ferraro and David Billingham. It has completed more than sixty building projects with clients including universities, charities, housing associations, local authorities and public companies. It maintains a team of designers, technicians and construction specialists and emphasises strong professional management and value for money.

Terry Farrell & Partners was set up after the dissolution of an earlier practice with Nicholas Grimshaw, and now has offices in London, Edinburgh and Hong Kong. The practice moved away from its earlier concerns with an architecture of services and structures, and made a name for itself in establishing a new approach to urban design that represented a complete break with modernist planning philosophy. During the course of the 1980s the practice grew through a series of major office development schemes; including buildings at Charing Cross, Alban Gate and Vauxhall Cross, which built on the post-modernist inspired approach to massing and detailing established with earlier, smaller buildings such as Henley Royal Regatta headquarters, TVam studios in Camden, and the Thames Water Authority building in Reading. More recently the practice has demonstrated a move away from this type of architecture towards a more high-tech approach in its competition-winning designs in Hong Kong, for the redevelopment of the Peak

Tower, the Headquarters for the British Consulate-General and the British Council, Kowloon Station on the Lantau Railway and the Kowloon Ventilation Building.

Feilden Clegg Architects is based in the Georgian city of Bath and maintains strong links with the School of Architecture and Engineering at Bath University. Thay have developed a reputation for environmentally-reponsive, sustainable architecture, often featuring timber construction. The practice is run as a cooperative out of an office in a listed stone brewery in Bath which it converted into five office suites, and won the 1992 Civic Trust Awards. Other work includes the headquarters for Greenpeace UK which was commended in the 1992 Green Buildings of the Year Awards, an environmental office and seminar block for the Building Research Establishment (1996), and the main entrance building for Open University in Milton Keynes. Among current projects are the Earth Centre in South Yorkshire for which the practice is masterplanning the preliminary stages and designing a gallery and entrance, and the Oxstalls Campus for Cheltenham & Gloucester College of Higher Education.

Foster and Partners is led by Sir Norman Foster with partners Spencer de Grey, David Nelson, Graham Phillips and Ken Shuttleworth. The three hundred-strong practice has evolved out of Foster Associates, established by Norman and Wendy Foster in 1967. It is now world-famous, with offices in Hong Kong, Berlin, Frankfurt, Glasgow and Tokyo. Sir Norman Foster has continually refined his approach through projects such as the Sainsbury Centre at the University of East Anglia, his own office building, the ITN building, the Sackler Galleries at the Royal Academy in London, and Stansted Airport in Essex. Today, the office's workload ranges from the largest construction project in the world, Chek Lap Kok airport in Hong Kong, to the design of a door handle, demonstrating their continuing commitment to detail. The practice has won more than one hundred and twenty five awards, but Foster stresses that many of these projects have developed out of tough commercial circumstances where time and money were the prime considerations. The office has an extensive network of Intergraph CAD workstations for design co-ordination, modelling, visualisation and rendering, as well as a team of twelve full-time model makers.

Future Systems is headed by two partners Jan Kaplicky and Amanda Levete, who had previously worked in the office of Richard Rogers. The practice's work has grown out of the high-tech tradition, but is fundamentally driven by a concern to address environmental issues, and to that end, it has always stressed the need to work closely with engineers. For many years the practice's work was widely published but largely theoretical, proposing innovative solutions, inspired both by natural forms and by the materials and technologies of the motor, aerospace, and boat industries. Each project challenges traditional preconceptions of architectural space and structure, as in the shortlisted competition proposal for the Tate's new gallery at Bankside, the Hauer-King house in north London, and the new media centre for Lord's Cricket Ground. The practice has been involved in two extensive environmental research programmes: a collaboration with Ove Arup & Partners, and a joint project with the Martin Centre at Cambridge University.

Nicholas Grimshaw and Partners was formed in 1980, and in 1982 won the Sports Council's competition for a design for a standardised sports hall – twenty-four of which have now been built across the UK. Grimshaw's architectural approach is firmly rooted in the British engineering tradition which, in the hands of Brunel and Paxton, became renowned worldwide. The practice is committed to the use of state-of-the-art building technology and materials to produce environmentally-responsive buildings. They have gained widespread publicity for the Financial Times printing works, the Camden Town Sainsbury store, and the International Passenger Terminal at Waterloo, a high-profile project which won the RIBA Building of the Year Award for 1994. Grimshaw and Partners designed the British Pavilion at the Seville Expo '92, which subsequently won seven awards. It is working on three landmark Millennium Commission-funded projects: the Eden Project in Cornwall, the National Space Science Centre in Leicester and the Millennium Point in Digbeth. The practice now has offices in London, Berlin and Manchester.

Zaha Hadid is an Iraqi-born, London-based architect who combines practice with teaching and research in the pursuit of an uncompromising commitment to modernism. She studied at the Architectural Association from 1972, winning the Diploma Prize in 1977. After the AA she joined the Dutch practice, OMA and then formed her own practice in 1979, winning world-wide recognition for her competition entry for the Peak, Hong Kong in 1983. This followed several first places in competitions for Kurfurstendamn, Berlin,1986, and Dusseldorf Art and Media Centre in 1989. The construction of a folly in Osaka and the Moonsoon restaurant in Japan established her highly individual design approach which is graphically represented in the office's dynamic and colourful paintings and drawings. In 1993, Hadid's distinctive fire station for the Vitra furniture company on the German/Swiss border opened to much acclaim, but the practice's triumphant victory in the Cardiff Bay Opera House competition in 1994 was subsequently soured by controversy, and the project is

not to be realised. Large-scale urban studies for harbour developments in Hamburg, Bordeaux and Cologne have been completed.

Herzog & de Meuron was formed in 1978 by Jacques Herzog and Pierre de Meuron. Both are currently visiting professors at Harvard University. Having completed a number of well-received, influential, but relatively small-scale projects in Switzerland, they achieved worldwide recognition when they were announced winners of the competition for the new Tate Gallery of Modern Art, Bankside, in London, in 1996. Their scheme for the under-stated conversion of the existing power station was welcomed by the competition assessors as successfully dealing with the architectural integrity of the building, and providing the most appropriate, neutral backdrop for showing contemporary art. Herzog and de Meuron's approach represents a contemporary re-interpretation of the modernist tradition, in which simplicity of form and function is infused with a controlled richness and warmth deriving from materials, surface texture, and details. Herzog & de Meuron are one of three practices shortlisted for the extension to the Museum of Modern Art, New York.

Hodder Associates is a Manchester and London-based practice which first attracted national attention in 1992 when their Colne Swimming Pool in Lancashire won the Royal Fine Art Commission/Sunday Times building of the year award. This resulted in their appointment to extend Arne Jacobsen's grade I listed St Catherine's College, Oxford. In 1994 they were selected as one of six practices to represent the emerging generation of British architects in an exhibition at the Architectural Institute of Japan, in Tokyo. In 1995 Hodder Associates received the grand prize at the Royal Academy summer exhibition for their entry in the Manchester City Art Gallery competition, and in 1996 it won the RIBA's inaugural Stirling Prize for Architecture for the Centenary Building at the University of Salford. Current projects range from the refurbishment of primary health care facilities to a £9 million leisure centre in London.

Michael Hopkins and Partners was formed in 1976, the three partners are Michael Hopkins, Patty Hopkins, and William Taylor. For many years their work has been dubbed "the acceptable face of modernism", combining modernist planning principles and a commitment to exploring new technologies with a sensitivity to site and place, a continuing interest in using traditional materials, and an openness to working in the context of historic buildings. In 1994, Michael and Patty Hopkins were jointly awarded the RIBA Gold Medal for Architecture. Some of the practice's earlier projects that received widespread attention were the architect's own house in north London and the circular factory for David

Mellor near Sheffield. Their conversion of Bracken House, originally designed by Albert Richardson, in the City of London, gained the practice plaudits from conservation groups and planners alike. In 1993 the practice won the major commission for the design and construction of the New Inland Revenue building in Nottingham. Most recently, Michael Hopkins and Partners completed a new music performance building for Emmanuel College, Cambridge.

Arata Isozaki & Associates was started in 1963 and was awarded Japan's Artist Newcomer Prize. Some of the practice's major buildings include: the Expo '70 Plaza in Osaka,1974; the Museum of Contemporary Art in Los Angeles,1986; the Olympic Stadium in Barcelona,1990; the Brooklyn Museum masterplan, the Kulturzentrum Art Tower, Mito, both in 1990; a concert hall in Kyoto, 1995, the Nara Convention Hall, 1996, and the Büro-gebäude at Potzdamer Platz, Berlin, 1997. In 1983 he won Japan's Mainichi Art Award. Arata Isozaki received the RIBA Gold Medal in 1986, and the Chicago Architecture Award in 1990.

Levitt Bernstein Associates was established in 1968. It is a practice which has long been associated with social projects such as housing, education and arts buildings, amongst which the Royal Exchange Theatre in Manchester, the Pier Arts Centre in Orkney, Royal Free Square housing in London, and King's Lynn Corn Exchange have all received awards. In the early 1990s they built their own free-standing office building in east London, which won the Office of the Year award, 1993. Levitt Bernstein Associates has always emphasised the importance of community consultation and client/user participation in the design process, and has developed special ways of managing these processes. It has also developed particular expertise in finding new uses for existing and historic buildings, and is a founder member of City Strategies, a multi-disciplinary consortium dealing with urban regeneration. The practice has eight directors, and an overall staff of eighty, including three landscape architects.

Daniel Libeskind established his architectural studio in Berlin in 1989. For many years, Libeskind was regarded primarily as a theoretical practitioner associated with the deconstructivist movement, pursuing a particular interest in developing design through reference to text, musical notation and philosophy. This is reflected in the recent decision of the American Academy of Arts and Letters to confer on him its Award for Architecture. Since setting up his practice in Berlin, they have benefitted from the building opportunities provided by the reunification of Germany. This has led to commissions for the planning and execution of city planning projects to link the former DDR's

urban fabric to the fast growing economy of Berlin. Libeskind's first, significant, built project was the extension to the Berlin Museum with the Jewish Museum. He recently won two competitions in Britain, for the Boilerhouse Extension to the Victoria & Albert Museum, London, and the Imperial War Museum of the North, in Manchester. He is also working on a scheme for the Bremen Philharmonic.

Lifschutz Davidson was formed in 1986 and operates from Hammersmith, west London, with a staff of twenty-five. The two partners previously worked for Richard Rogers, and the practice's work generates imaginative solutions to problems of architectural structure and services. The first project to attract media interest was their rooftop extension to Rogers' riverside office building, and since then the practice has grown rapidly. Its varied work includes private and community housing, super-markets, a power station, a railway station for London's planned Crossrail, offices, bridges and, currently a large urban improve-ment scheme for London's South Bank.

Jose Ignacio Linazasoro arquitecto completed two major works in the Basque country, the Basque school in Hondarribia,1974-8 with Miguel Garay, and the reconstruction of the monastery of Carmelite Nuns in San Sebastian,1983–91. Other major works are the University Library in Madrid,1988–94, and, most recently, the restoration and extension of the former Hospital del Rey at Melilla on the north-east coast of Morocco. The practice won first prizes in the competitions for the Spanish Pavilion at Expo '92 in Seville, the 1989 international competition for the precincts of Reims Cathedral, and the 1996 competition for urban renewal and a new cultural centre in Lavapies, Madrid.

MacCormac Jamieson Prichard was formed in 1972, and is based in east London, with a staff of fifty architects. The practice has strong links with Oxford and Cambridge Universities, for whom it has built a number of collegiate buildings, and it is currently working on a masterplan for the expansion of Cambridge University. The practice's use of mainly traditional materials and planning concepts, and its respect for cultural and physical context, led to an increasing number of projects for historically sensitive locations, such as an office development near St Paul's Cathedral at Paternoster Square. Other major projects include the training college for Cable & Wireless, the Jubilee Line Exten-sion tube station at Southwark, the pedestrianisation of the London School of Economics campus. Projects currently in hand include the Wellcome Wing for London's Science Museum and the Ruskin Library at Lancaster University. Richard MacCormac was President of the RIBA from 1990–92, where he was respon sible for setting up the Architecture Centre's exhbition and lecture programme.

David Marks Julia Barfield Architects is a young award-winning practice with an innovative, environmentally aware and humanistic approach. Its two most prestigious projects are the Millennium Wheel and the Weather-Watch Discovery Centre funded by the Millennium Commission. The British Airways Millennium Wheel is a 500-foot diameter Ferris wheel to be built on the banks of the River Thames opposite the Houses of Parliament which, for five years from 1999, will offer millions of visitors spectacular views of the city. The Weather-Watch Discovery Centre, in Bracknell, Berkshire, home of the Meteorological Office is intended to provide a dramatic new symbol for the town. It will consist of an 80-metre-high stainless steel tower and an children's interactive educational centre.

José Rafael Moneo qualified as an architect in 1961 in Madrid and has since combined practice with teaching. He has a strong reputation as a theoretician and critic, but has also completed a substantial body of building work, including the Diestre Factory, Zarogoza,1967, National Museum of Roman Art, Merida, 1986, the San Pablo Airport , Seville, 1992, the Atocha Railway Station, Madrid, 1992, and the Davies Art Museum, Massachusetts,1993. Work now under construction includes the Barcelona Concert Hall, the Museum of Modern Art & Architecture, Stockholm, and the Potsdamer Platz hotel and office building, Berlin. Rafael Moneo was the chair of the architecture department at Harvard University's graduate school of design from 1985–1990, and in 1996 he was awarded both the Pritzker Prize and International Union of Architects Gold Medal. Moneo represents one of the most prominent figures in the Spanish architectural renaissance of the last two decades, which successfully fuses a pared-down approach deriving from Modernism with a richness and inventiveness drawn from a more flexible contemporary re-interpretation of that tradition.

Dominique Perrault started his career at the Atelier Parisien d'Urbanisme (APUR) in 1981, the organisation originally set up to oppose Corbusian plans for the redevelopment of Paris and protect the city's historic fabric. He began to enter competitions at the same time, benefitting from the French government's active programme of promotion for young architects. In 1981 he won the Programme d'architecture nouvelle XII, and opened his own office in Paris. He established his reputation in France with an engineering school in Marne-la-Vallée,1984–7, and the industrial Hôtel Berlier in the 13th district of Paris,1986–90. But it was in 1989 that he shot to international attention when he won the

design competition for the Bibliothèque de France, one of the last of President Mitterrand's *grands projets* in Paris. The controversial scheme, which opened in 1996, is typical of Perrault's liking for grand formal gestures, and an interesting range of materials and textures. In the wake of this project he won the competition for the Olympic velodrome and swimming pool in Berlin in 1992, and opened an office in Berlin. He won the French National Award for Architecture in 1993 and the Mies van der Rohe award for European architecture in 1997.

Christian de Portzamparc studied architecture at the Ecole Normale Supérieure des Beaux-Arts, Paris. In the 1970s Portzamparc designed a new dance school for the Paris Opera and a housing scheme in the Rue Nationale which attracted considerable attention. In 1981 his work *The Presence of the Past*, organised by Paolo Portoghesi to celebrate the influence of post-modernism on architecture, was exhibited at the Venice Biennale. Portzamparc opposes the metal and glass "architecture of transparency" promoted by certain practitioners in France. In the late 1980s he won the competition to design the last of Mitterrand's *grands projets* in Paris, the City of Music. This is his largest project to date, built in two phases and completed in 1996. In 1994 his international contribution to architecture was recognised by being awarded the Pritzker Prize.

Pringle Richards Sharratt Architects was formed in London in 1996 by directors John Pringle, Penny Richards and Ian Sharratt. Pringle and Sharratt were previously partners with Michael Hopkins & Partners, working on projects such as Lord's Cricket Ground, the Inland Revenue Centre, Nottingham, and the New Parliamentary Building at Westminster. Richards had her own practice which gained a reputation in museum design, projects including the Glass Gallery at the Victoria & Albert Museum. Since forming the practice, projects have included the redevelopment of Bastion House (a 17-storey office building above the Museum of London), the masterplan for the Victoria & Albert Museum, a sports building for Middlesex University, the V & A Millennium Gallery and Winter-Garden, Sheffield and a masterplan for South Bank University.

Ian Ritchie Architects was established in 1981 in London, and now has a staff of twenty and liaison offices in Paris (Rice Francis Ritchie, an engineering practice set up with the late Peter Rice) and Berlin. Ritchie's work has always been linked with that particular brand of British architecture rooted in a sophisticated structural engineering tradition. Notable projects include the Louvre sculpture courts and pyramids (with I.M. Pei), the Ecology Gallery at the Natural History Museum, B8 offices at

Stockley Park, London, and the Crystal Palace concert platform, London. Current projects include Bermondsey underground station and the Royal Albert Dock Rowing Centre, both in London; WaterWorld Leisure Centre in County Cork; plus competition-winning designs for new electricity pylons and the Terrasson Cultural Greenhouse in France, in collaboration with the landscape designer Kathryn Gustavson. Ritchie's work has been widely published and exhibited, and his own book, *(well) Connected Architecture* was published in 1994. He is a fellow of the Royal Society of Arts, chairman of EEC Europan UK, and visiting professor at the Technical University Vienna.

Richard Rogers Partnership was founded in 1977 by Richard Rogers, John Young, Marco Goldschmied and Mike Davies and now has a hundred-strong office with almost half its commissions overseas. Richard Rogers has firmly consolidated his position as a highly influential figure in the British architectural establishment, and along with Foster, with whom he originally founded Team 4 in the 1960s, as one of the world's best-known architects. Rogers' success was founded on his early victory in winning the competition for the new Pompidou Centre in Paris (with Renzo Piano), a radical scheme in the midst of one of the city's most historic districts, in which the services of the building are deliberately displayed on the outside. This was followed by the Lloyd's Building in the City of London. Subsequently, the partnership has continued to explore the sophisticated aesthetic expression of advanced technical solutions to construction and servicing problems through a range of projects which have progressively increased in scale and size. Many of the practice's projects have been corporate headquarters and office buildings, but current projects include designs for Heathrow's fifth terminal, the redevelopment of London's South Bank Centre arts complex, and the Millennium Dome exhibition centre in Greenwich. Prizes include the International Union of Architects August Perret Prize for most outstanding international work and RIBA Awards for Lloyd's building; Reuters building in Docklands; Channel 4 Headquarters; Thames Reach Housing, Billingsgate Fish Market restoration, and Linn Products, while Richard Rogers himself received the RIBA Gold Medal in 1985, was knighted in 1991 and received a peerage in 1996.

Sauerbruch Hutton Architects is the Anglo-German partnership of Louisa Hutton and Matthias Sauerbruch, who both trained at the Architectural Association in London. Matthias Sauerbruch went on to work for a time with the Dutch practice OMA, before establishing a practice with Hutton in London in 1987. In 1992 they set up a Berlin office on winning an international competition to design a new corporate headquarters building, currently

under construction. The practice identifies with the aims and ideals of the modern movement, and strives to produce an architecture which effortlessly responds to the high degree of complexity found in the contemporary urban situation. Instead of conventional urban strategies, they propose hybrid structures which tend to combine aspects of both city and country. They regard the reunification of Berlin as a specific challenge and source of inspiration, as well as a case study for the future of European cities, and their work resists attempts to re-establish a more traditional, historicist approach to city-planning, which they regard as inappropriate to contemporay conditions.

Stanton Williams was formed in 1986 by Alan Stanton and Paul Williams, who had formerly worked in exhibition design at the Victoria and Albert Museum. Their early work consisted mainly of exhibitions, installations and interior projects, in which they demonstrated an increasingly refined and sophisticated approach to handling light, space and materials using a minimal palette of materials. The elegant understatement of their architectural aesthetic, articulated by an intense concern for detail and craftsmanship, led to their winning their first public commission for a shop for Issey Miyake in London 1987. During the 1990s, the practice has steadily grown in size and in the scale of its work. Completed London projects include: the Design Museum,1989; Classic FM studios,1992; The Old Royal Observatory, Greenwich, 1993; and the Osho Gallery,1993. Outside London it has designed the Gas Hall, Birmingham,1993, the Ashmolean Museum, Oxford 1995, and Compton Verney, Warwickshire 1997. Current projects include the Millennium Seed Bank and Visitor Centre at Wakehurst Place, Sussex, and alterations to the Royal National Theatre, London.

Studio E Architects was founded in 1994 by David Lloyd Jones and Cezary Bednarski. Studio E's projects and studies include a pioneering solar energy-powered office building, an energy-efficient head-office and distribution centre, structures and facilities for Garsington Opera, twenty temporary hotel bridges in Rome for the Anno Santo 2000, a landmark structure for the Museum of the Moving Image and National Theatre in London, designed in collaboration with light artist Peter Fink, as well as studies covering the integration of photovoltaics in buildings. The practice is also patron supplier of architectural and design services to the Restaurateurs Association of Great Britain.

Michael Wilford and Partners was formed after the death of Sir James Stirling, in 1992. The original practice, James Stirling, Michael Wilford and Associates was founded on the success of the Leicester University Engineering Building designed by

Stirling and James Gowan in 1958–63, and the History Faculty Library at Cambridge University of 1967–8. The partnership between Wilford and Stirling was established in 1971, and in 1977 the practice won a major competition for the new Staatsgalerie in Stuttgart, Germany. This project seemed to represent a considerable change from the practice's modernist, brutalist credentials, in its overt historical references and distinctively post-modernist approach. It was followed in a similar vein by the Clore Gallery extension to the Tate in London, and an alternative scheme, memorably described by the Prince of Wales as looking like a '30s wireless, commissioned by Peter Palumbo for the site at the Mansion House in the City of London. Since the death of Stirling, Wilford has completed a project for the Temasek Polytechnic in Singapore, and is working on schemes for the Philharmonic Hall in Los Angeles, the Kyoto Centre in Japan, and a railway station in Bilbao. These projects signify a move away from Stirling's flirtation with post-modernism towards a more high-tech form of expression.

Chris Wilkinson Architects was established in 1983. The practice has developed an approach based on an informed use of technology combined with a love of art, engineering and all aspects of design. Over the last three years they have become particularly well-known for designing bridges, winning five major competitions for new bridges, and transportation projects, including the Stratford Market depot for London's Jubilee Line extension, in east London, which won several awards. Chris Wilkinson Architects are now working on a new station at Stratford, due for completion in 1998, and the Millennium project for a science centre in Bristol, the main production and research facility for James Dyson's cyclonic vacuum cleaners, and two new galleries for London's Science Museum. The practice won the Royal Academy's AJ/Bovis Grand Award in 1997 and was the Chartered Society of Designers designer of the year in 1996.

Colin St John Wilson and Partners was founded in Cambridge in 1965, but relocated to London in 1969 and is most famous now for its twenty-year project to design and build the new British Library at St Pancras, London. St John Wilson's practice has been consistently informed by intellectual concerns, reflecting his time as Professor and Head of the Department of Architecture at Cambridge University from 1975–1989, and in 1992 he published a book of selected writings, *Architectural Reflections*. He has retained a love of and commitment to the precepts of Scandivanian modernism as practised by Alvar Aalto, which exerted a strong influence on the Cambridge School in the '50s and '60s under Sir Leslie Martin, with whom St John Wilson ran a practice from 1956 to 1964. St John Wilson's involvement with the British

Library project has led to a number of other commissions for library buildings, including one for Queen Mary College in London, the Bishop Wilson Memorial Library in Springfield, Essex, and the Chicago Public Library with executive architects Beeby Babka.